How To Use Social Norms Marketing To Prevent Driving After Drinking

A MOST of Us Toolkit

Jeffrey W. Linkenbach, Ed.D.

A publication of MOST of Us at Montana State University-Bozeman

www.mostofus.org

ISBN 0-9770446-0-2

Library of Congress Control Number: 2005936549

Printed in the United States of America

MOST of Us® is a registered trademark of Montana State University-Bozeman

100% of the revenue from this book is dedicated to future health and safety learning, discovery, and outreach.

Book design and layout by Maxwell Design - Bozeman, Montana

TABLE OF CONTENTS

Welcome to the MOST of Us Toolkit.

What you have in your hands is more than a book. It is an invitation to transform the way that you conduct your prevention and safety work. The MOST of Us model of social norms marketing is one of the most rewarding ways of preventing injury and loss of life that I have discovered in my 20-year history as a researcher and practitioner.

By engaging in this process, you have the opportunity to change your work and the way you see the world. By focusing on identifying and changing the misperceptions of others, you will begin to notice the ways in which your own perceptions are skewed. You may also discover that we have often conducted safety programs backwards. When you begin to work with the social norms approach, you will see that the way we tend to focus on the problem—especially in the media—may be actually contributing to the very misperceptions that we seek to correct. You will notice that the hidden risk factor of misperceptions operates at many levels.

During the MOST of Us process you will experience success and failure. Both, I say, are great! It is only by jumping in and getting started that you can learn how to apply this model and become successful at reducing driving after drinking in your community or state. The learning curve may be steep, but the rewards are worth it: saving lives, reducing risks, preventing injuries, improving health. It does not get any better than that.

I wrote this book to assist you with your efforts. In return, I hope that as you discover new tips and tools you will share them with me and with other traffic safety practitioners through our online community at *communities.mostofus.org*. We benefit when we learn from each other.

Best of luck in your efforts.

Sincerely,

Dr. Jeffrey Linkenbach
Director
MOST of Us

WHO IS MOST OF US?

MOST of Us is a nonprofit, full-service social norms marketing and research firm based at Montana State University–Bozeman. Since it was founded in 1998, MOST of Us has pioneered new uses of the social norms approach and conducted award-winning health promotion campaigns. MOST of Us conducted the first statewide application of social norms marketing, and initiated the use of social norms with the issues of tobacco and seatbelt use on a wide scale. As a recognized leader in the field, MOST of Us is committed to expanding the application and success of our methodology to benefit the health, safety, and welfare of the public.

In addition to conducting our own research, MOST of Us serves as a national center for planning, implementing and evaluating social norms programs in communities, schools, and other settings. MOST of Us can be contracted to provide technical assistance on or to carry out:

- **environmental advocacy**
- **strategic planning**
- **fundraising, budgeting, and grants planning**
- **survey design**
- **survey administration**
- **message selection**
- **market research and planning**
- **advertising and media creation**
- **media placement**
- **program and staff development**
- **program evaluation**

MOST of Us has also become a leader in creating technology that streamlines, simplifies and increases the scope of health promotion efforts. MOST of Us has developed a suite of online tools designed precisely for those who work in health promotion. These tools—which include our cutting-edge survey system, communication and file sharing network, and interactive learning modules—are designed to be secure, reliable, easy to use, and budget-friendly.

MOST of Us knows that the field is advanced when social norms researchers and practitioners are in contact with one another. For this reason, we have created the Social Norms Network Community and made it available free of charge. Join this online network at **communities.mostofus.org** and share information, give and receive technical assistance, and learn from what others are doing.

In 1998, MOST of Us hosted the first annual National Conference on the Social Norms Model, which brought key practitioners and researchers together. We continue this cutting-edge discovery each year at the Montana Summer Institute for Social Norms Practitioners, where we explore the newest frontiers of social norms research and practice.

To find out more about working with MOST of Us, using MOST of Us technologies, or attending the Montana Summer Institute for Social Norms Practitioners, please visit our website at **mostofus.org**, write to mail@mostofus.org, or call (406) 994-7873.

Social norms is an innovative, science-based approach to health promotion that has a demonstrated track record of changing perceptions, attitudes and behaviors in a variety of target groups across an increasingly broad range of issues, including driving after drinking (Berkowitz, 2004). Of course, no single strategy is a "magic bullet;" driving after drinking is a complex issue that requires a comprehensive, multi-pronged approach.

MOST of Us Tip: Expand Your Efforts

This Toolkit contains specific information and examples related to the prevention of driving after drinking, but most of the material it contains could be used to plan a social norms campaign on virtually any topic.

Social norms campaigns come in all shapes and sizes. They can be statewide behemoths with budgets in the millions, or they can be individual community programs that operate entirely on donated resources. This Toolkit will help you plan and implement a social norms program in your state, region, town or community—whatever size program you have in mind. This Toolkit can also be used as a step-by-step training curriculum for a workshop or seminar on social norms programs.

HOW TO USE THIS TOOLKIT

1) Open front cover.
2) Read, with breaks for food, water, and unmentionables.
3) Use the "MOST of Us Tips," which highlight lessons MOST of Us has learned from the many social norms campaigns we have run, including the MOST of Us Prevent Drinking and Driving Campaign.

SOCIAL NORMS: A NEW APPROACH TO PREVENTION

The social norms approach to prevention emerged as a way of explaining and shaping human behavior based upon the powerful role of perceptions (Perkins and Berkowitz, 1986). Social norms theory maintains that people's behavior is strongly influenced by their perceptions of the attitudes and behaviors of their peers. If people think harmful behavior is "typical," they are more likely to engage in it. If they think protective behavior is the norm, then that type of behavior holds sway. For example, if individuals hold an exaggerated idea of the acceptance or frequency of driving after drinking among their peers, they are more likely to experiment with or increase their own risky driving after drinking behavior.

The key to the behavior-changing potential of the social norms approach is that most people misperceive the normative behavior of their peers. Social norms studies have repeatedly found that people think risk-taking behavior is more prevalent than it actually is (Perkins, 2003). Further, social norms research has shown that if people's misperceptions are corrected to reflect the actual, less risky, more protective behaviors and attitudes that are the norm in their communities, they are more likely to behave in accordance with those positive standards (Cialdini, 2003; Perkins, 1997, 2003).

KEY SOCIAL NORMS TERMS

Social norms are simply the behaviors or attitudes of the majority of people in any community or group. If most people in a community do not smoke, then not smoking is the "normative" behavior, or the social norm. Not smoking is normal, acceptable, and perhaps even expected in that population.

Perceptions of social norms are people's beliefs about the norms of their peers. Perceptions of social norms play an important role in shaping our individual behavior. Our perceptions of acceptable, majority behavior—how fast we think "most people" drive, whether we think "most people" wear seatbelts, how many drinks we think "most people" have before getting behind the wheel—help shape our own behavioral decisions. People often misperceive the social norms of their peers, thinking that risky behavior occurs with far greater frequency and social acceptance than it actually does.

Consequences of misperceptions of social norms. People tend to behave in the way they believe is typical and accepted. If people believe that risky behaviors are typical, they are more likely to engage in those behaviors. First, people may be more likely to take part in a high-risk activity if they misperceive it as the norm. Second, those who regularly engage in high-risk activities will wrongly think that their behavior is accepted social practice. And third, fear of social disapproval can make people reluctant to intervene to stop dangerous behaviors that they believe are socially sanctioned.

THE SCIENCE OF THE POSITIVE VS. HEALTH TERRORISM

Most of us prevent drinking and driving. Most of us wear seatbelts. Most of us are tobacco- and drug-free. In fact, most of us make positive decisions about our health and safety (Malenfant, Wells, Van Houten and Williams, 1996; Linkenbach and Perkins, 2003a, 2003b; Perkins and Craig, 2003). That is the norm.

But in most prevention campaigns, the healthy behavior and attitudes of the majority are ignored. Instead, prevention specialists, health educators and activists attempt to "scare the health" into people using threats, alarming information, and horrifying images. This "health terrorist" (Linkenbach, 2001) strategy is based on the belief that people can be frightened into making healthier choices. From a social norms perspective, however, this strategy can work to increase risky behaviors by supporting the misperception that they are practiced by the majority.

Unlike health terrorism, social norms theory is built upon the "science of the positive" (Linkenbach, 1999, 2003). Social norms campaigns focus on the healthy behavior of the majority, employing images and messages that accurately reflect their positive norms without, of course, denying or diminishing the threat that the risk-taking minority poses to us all. By highlighting and amplifying the positive attitudes and behavior of the majority, more such attitudes and behaviors result.

HOW A SOCIAL NORMS CAMPAIGN WORKS

In short, a social norms campaign works like this:

Baseline Survey
Collect information on your target audience's actual behavior and attitudes as compared to their perceptions of the behavior and attitudes of their peers.

Campaign Implementation
Expose your audience to high levels of a perception-correcting intervention.

Perception Correction
Audience develops more accurate perceptions of their peers' behavioral and attitudinal norms.

Behavior/Attitude Change
A larger percentage of your target audience acts in accordance with positive community norms.

THE MOST OF US PREVENT DRINKING AND DRIVING CAMPAIGN

MOST of Us learned many lessons about running an intervention to reduce driving after drinking from our MOST of Us Prevent Drinking and Driving Campaign. Conducted statewide from 2001 to 2003 for the Montana Department of Transportation and the National Highway Traffic Safety Administration, this effort successfully reduced self-reported rates of driving after drinking among Montana's young adults, ages 21 to 34. Information and insight gained during this campaign is included throughout this Toolkit.

The campaign began with a baseline survey, which showed that 79.6% of Montana young adults had not driven within one hour of consuming two or more drinks in the previous month. However, 92% of the survey respondents perceived that the majority of their peers had. Such a disparity between perception and behavior is precisely what social norms theory predicts, and by correcting this misperception, the MOST of Us Prevent Drinking and Driving Campaign was able to reduce the prevalence of drinking and driving among its target audience, as measured by self-reported survey data.

WHAT MAKES A DRIVER "IMPAIRED?"

There are various definitions of alcohol impairment. All states now use a Blood Alcohol Content (BAC) of .08% or less as the legal limit for drivers. The National Highway Traffic Safety Administration defines impairment as any amount of alcohol in a driver's system. Be cautious about the terms you use—you don't want to use the term "impairment" in a way that conflicts with the laws of your state. Even if you collect data on the number of drinks people have within a given amount of time, you cannot know for sure if they were legally impaired. It is best to use another term, such as "driving after drinking" that you can define to meet the parameters of your survey and campaign.

MOST of Us then carried out a 15-month intervention in 15 counties in western Montana. These intervention counties were exposed to high doses of the social norms message via paid radio and television commercials, local and college newspaper advertisements, theater slides, posters, billboards, and promotional items. The remainder of the state acted as a low-dosage control area, and was exposed only to low levels of free media. All of this media communicated the normative message that, **"MOST Montana Young Adults (4 out of 5) Don't Drink and Drive."**

MOST of Us conducted three follow-up surveys at points during and after the campaign. In each survey, respondents were asked identical questions about their attitudes, behaviors and perceptions about driving after drinking. These surveys showed that, by the end of the campaign, young adults in the intervention counties were more accurately seeing the normative environment than their counterparts in the control counties. Specifically, the results among young adults in the intervention counties compared with those in the control counties showed:

- A 7.5% relative decrease in the percentage who believed that the average Montanan their age drove after drinking during the previous month

- An 11.0% relative increase in the percentage who accurately perceived that the majority of their peers use non-drinking designated drivers
- A 16.5% relative increase in the percentage who would support passing a law to decrease the Blood Alcohol Content (BAC) legal limit for driving to .08%

From this data, MOST of Us concluded that the high-intensity social norms campaign carried out in the intervention counties corrected the target audience's misperceptions of drinking and driving norms. Further, the correction of their misperception of drinking and driving norms increased their healthy attitudes and behaviors, as measured in the follow-up surveys. The final survey results showed:

- A 13.7% relative decrease in the percentage who reported driving after drinking
- A 15.0% relative increase in the percentage who reported always using non-drinking designated drivers

For more information on the MOST of Us Prevent Drinking and Driving Campaign, see NHTSA publication DOT HS 809 869, the detailed report on the project published by the the National Highway Traffic Safety Administration.

MOST of Us Tip: One Size Does Not Fit All

This guide sets out a campaign strategy based upon the most current research in the field and extensive MOST of Us campaign experience. It is not, however, a foolproof recipe for success. Each campaign will have specific needs and challenges that this guide cannot anticipate or address. The tools you choose will depend upon the goals of your campaign and the resources you can devote to achieving them.

THE MONTANA MODEL OF SOCIAL NORMS MARKETING

The Montana Model of Social Norms Marketing (Linkenbach, 2003) is a seven-step process that combines social marketing with the social norms approach to prevention. The Montana Model is a process for turning social science into social action by correcting misperceptions and building upon the positive attitudinal and behavioral norms that already exist in a culture.

The Montana Model can work on local, regional or statewide levels for a variety of issues. It has been the foundation of successful MOST of Us campaigns on topics ranging from driving after drinking among young adults, to tobacco use among teenagers to adult seatbelt use.

This Toolkit is organized around the seven-step Montana Model. As you read on, remember that while the steps are presented in a linear manner, their implementation is a dynamic process that often involves operating within and between each of the steps simultaneously.

Montana Model
of Social Norms Marketing

The Montana Model - Dr. Linkenbach, 1999

14

PLANNING AND ENVIRONMENTAL ADVOCACY

Project planning determines the scope and direction of your campaign, and ensures that all of your efforts are aligned with your program goals. Environmental advocacy entails creating a political, economic and social atmosphere conducive to change.

STEP 1.1 ENVIRONMENTAL ADVOCACY

Environmental advocacy is the process of creating a political, economic and social atmosphere that is supportive of your campaign and its goals. This step can be quite time-consuming, but it is essential and should not be skimped on.

Explain "The Science of the Positive"

Social norms is a new and sometimes controversial approach to prevention. Social norms campaigns challenge people's commonly-held perceptions about the environments they live in and the behavior of their peers, as well as their beliefs about how problems like driving after drinking should be confronted. You can improve the reception of your campaign, and reduce the inevitable criticism of it, if you educate key stakeholders and community members about social norms theory and win their support for your campaign before it begins.

To help people better understand and accept social norms, it can be helpful to frame it within the larger context of what MOST of Us likes to call "The Science of the Positive" (Linkenbach, 1999, 2003). Social norms is a way to approach issues from a positive rather than a negative perspective. It is a move away from the "if it bleeds, it leads" sensational-ization of issues by the media. Social norms and "the science of the positive" hold that people's behavior can be shaped through positive modeling and reinforcement, rather than through threats and punishment.

Reduce the Noise of the Negative

Try to reduce the number of negative, fear-based messages that could dilute the impact of your campaign. Fear-based media efforts compete with positive social norms messages by solidifying already-exaggerated misperceptions about the prevalence of driving after drinking. Your campaign will have much greater power for change if you can turn down the volume of potentially competitive messages and expose your target audience to consistent, pervasive messages about healthy behaviors and attitudes being the norm.

Work with your local traffic safety office, prevention groups and coalitions to withhold "health terrorism" during the duration of your intervention. Try to convince them to put their campaigns on hold or to run only compatible, positive messages (which you might even offer to help them create). This can be a valuable opportunity to find common ground with law enforcement and other prevention groups.

Develop Relationships with Key Stakeholders

Key stakeholders are people and organizations who can influence your target population and help or hinder your campaign. Examples include government agency officials, law enforcement officers, substance abuse treatment professionals, educators, and the media.

To identify your key stakeholders, ask yourself these questions:

? Who has a vested interest in the operation of your campaign?

? Who are the people/agencies that could support (or thwart) your campaign?

? Which agencies and individuals will support the goals of your campaign?

? Which people/agencies are important for communication and publicity?

? Who can you partner with to help legitimize your campaign?

? Who could provide additional resources or in-kind (non-monetary) support?

? Who could help sustain your campaign beyond your initial funding?

? Who are the "secondary reinforcers" of your campaign message? Who is sending out a competing or conflicting message?

MOST of Us Tip: Build Stakeholder Support

Some of your key stakeholders may be skeptical of the social norms approach. Educating them and winning their support for your campaign is crucial. Call your stakeholders, send an introductory mailing, and spend time talking with them about your campaign. Good communication with key stakeholders can help build recognition and support for your campaign, and open up opportunities for valuable partnerships.

Pre-Campaign Media Advocacy

Pre-campaign media advocacy is your opportunity to set the stage for your campaign by pitching stories that put your campaign in context and frame driving after drinking from the social norms perspective. This work will prepare the media, key stakeholders, your target audience and the larger community for your campaign before it begins, and will reduce the chance that your messages will be misunderstood.

Contact your local media outlets. Introduce yourself and your campaign, and pitch stories that stress the importance of the positive approach. Picture headlines like "Traffic Safety Researchers Try New Approach" or "A Fresh Take on Driving After Drinking."

Feel free to provide a "teaser" of the campaign to come by sharing messages, images or other materials that you have ready. Try to book yourself on local radio and TV talk shows—the more ways you can prepare your community for your campaign, the better.

Finally, help your campaign staff and key stakeholders respond to questions from the media. Provide them with speaking points so that your statements about the campaign are consistent and the issue is consistently framed in a positive way.

For more information about working with the media, please see Step 6 or download "The Main Frame" from **mostofus.org**.

STEP 1.2 *SETTING CAMPAIGN GOALS*

The most important thing to remember about goal-setting is this: The goals you establish for your campaign must be achievable by correcting misperceptions of norms.

Most people know that by driving drunk they risk killing or injuring themselves or someone else. In fact, NHTSA surveys have shown that Americans consider driving after drinking a more pressing social issue than health care, poverty or education. The goal of increasing awareness of the dangers of driving after drinking is therefore not an appropriate goal for a social norms campaign, since people do not generally misperceive the threat posed by this behavior.

Make sure that you do not set out to correct misperceptions that might work in your favor. For example, if people in your community have an exaggerated idea of the risk of getting pulled over for driving while impaired, it would undermine your prevention effort to inform them that the actual chances of arrest are lower than they think.

Your goal or goals should be:

- Clear and concise
- Achievable in scope (don't set out to eliminate driving after drinking in 18 months)
- Achievable in number (having too many goals with inadequate resources is a recipe for failure)
- Complementary (your goals should work together, not compete)

☑ State *who* you want to change

☑ State *what* you want to change

☑ State *how much* change you want to achieve

☑ Establish the *time period* during which you want the change to take place

These goals will be your mission statement, providing focus and clarity for everything you do. Check that your campaign materials and activities are consistent with your goals.

EXAMPLE GOALS

Driving after drinking is a complex problem. Depending upon which elements of the issue are most critical in your intervention area—and what type of change you will be able to accurately measure— you may want to focus on reducing the number of alcohol-related crashes, reducing self-reported rates of high-risk drinking, or increasing self-reported use of protective behaviors such as the use of designated drivers.

Goal: To reduce the self-reported frequency of driving after drinking in western Montana by 5% after a one-year social norms marketing campaign.

Goal: To increase support among Denver's young adults for passage of a .08 BAC legal limit for drivers by 10% after a six-month campaign.

Goal: To increase self-reported use of designated drivers among 21- to 34-year-olds in southern Ohio by 15% after a two-year media campaign.

STEP 1.3 *SETTING CAMPAIGN OBJECTIVES*

Campaign objectives are precise, measurable actions that support the achievement of your campaign goals, such as designing a survey, administering the survey, developing a campaign message and a market plan, delivering the message through media, and conducting post-test surveys. Your objectives are the criteria for tracking your progress and evaluating your program's success. If you accomplish all of your objectives in order, the result should be successful implementation of your campaign goals.

Your objectives should be:

☑ Clearly written

✓ Precisely defined

✓ Realistic and attainable

✓ Easily communicated to funders, staff and others involved in your project

✓ Charted with staff responsibilities and target completion dates

---

EXAMPLE OBJECTIVES

1. Gather baseline survey data through a phone survey of the target population. Collect information on self-reported DUI risk and protective behaviors, as well as perceptions of the normative environment.

2. Develop campaign messages based upon phone survey results.

3. Conduct market analysis and develop a market plan for changing the perceptions and behaviors of the target population. The market plan will deliver maximum awareness of the social norms messages to the target group, based upon budget.

4. Pilot-test campaign materials with target population and key stakeholders.

5. Deliver two 10-week media flights based upon the market plan.

6. Conduct post-test surveys of the target population to evaluate changes in reported perceptions, attitudes, and behaviors.

7. Write up methodology and results in document to be provided to funders.

STEP 1.4 *SELECTING YOUR TARGET AUDIENCE*

According to social norms theory, a high-risk environment is defined as one in which misperceptions of norms are widespread. Over the past few years, the growing volume of social norms research has shown that misperceptions occur in multiple populations (children, teens, college students, adults) and across a wide range of issues (smoking, alcohol and other drug use, driving after drinking) (Perkins, 2003; Berkowitz, 2004). The exact nature and degree of misperceptions among your target audience will be revealed by your baseline survey.

For help defining your target audience, look to your campaign goals. If your goal is to reduce the frequency of alcohol-related crashes, you may want to focus on the age and/or gender group that is responsible for the greatest number of alcohol-related crashes in your state.

Be as specific as possible: define your target in terms of age, gender, and place of work or residence. No matter what type of budget you have to work with, you can identify a target population (people living in certain regions, counties, towns, or communities) that you have the resources to reach. The thoughtfulness and precision with which you determine your target audience is one factor determining whether or not your campaign will achieve results.

MOST of Us Tip: The Law is The Law

Consider the potential political difficulties of including youth younger than 21 in your target group. The issue of underage drinking can be a political minefield. Prevention professionals and members of the community often react negatively to a campaign that attempts to reduce underage driving after drinking, which they may misperceive as tacit acceptance (or worse, encouragement) of underage drinking. Any campaign targeted at those under 21 years old should include a disclaimer such as "Any amount of alcohol may be illegal or dangerous" in all of its messages and materials.

If you do want to include—or even concentrate on—underage drinkers, be aware of the context of conflict in which your campaign will be embedded. Take pains to involve and get buy-in from your stakeholders, then stay on target, focusing on reducing misperceptions to achieve your goals.

CULTURAL CATARACTS

We as a society have cultural cataracts (Linkenbach, 2001). Our vision is distorted by the media's "if it bleeds, it leads" focus on the problems and harm caused by the dangerous behavior of a small percentage of people. Instead of fostering cultural conditions that nurture and support healthy behavior, the media obsessively focuses on problems, risk, and danger, fueling even more exaggerated perceptions of their prevalence. As a result, we have developed negative perceptions of certain subpopulations, including teens, college students and young adults. Social norms campaigns work to refocus our vision on the positive, healthy behavior that is the norm among these communities. Data from social norms interventions demonstrate that messages and images that portray health as the normative, expected behavior result in increased health protections and lowered risk (Haines, 1996).

STEP 1.5 *CHOOSING INTERVENTION AND CONTROL AREAS*

Ideally, you will set your campaign up as a controlled experiment, which will best allow you to measure the impact of your efforts. The **intervention area** is the area that you will saturate with your campaign message to change the perceptions and behavior of your target audience.

The **control area** must be kept free of your campaign materials; it will serve as the standard of comparison showing which, if any, of the changes that you measure in your intervention area might have occurred even in the absence of your campaign. You should carry out identical baseline and follow-up surveys in both areas; comparison of these results will serve as a measure of your campaign's effectiveness.

WHY HAVE INTERVENTION AND CONTROL AREAS?

A controlled experiment measures the effects of an intervention by comparing treated subjects (e.g. a population exposed to your campaign message) with a "control group" who do not receive the treatment. Except for the running of your campaign, conditions in the two areas should be as uniform as possible.

A controlled experiment allows you to:

1. Measure the impacts of a single change agent: your social norms campaign.

2. Confirm that the change you measure in your target population is attributable to your campaign, and not to some other factor.

3. Identify which changes might have happened even in the absence of your campaign.

4. Increase the scientific rigor of your intervention. This will allow you to carry out more sophisticated statistical analyses of your results, and will make your campaign one that adds to the body of data about the efficacy of the social norms approach.

Locating and selecting two demographically matched sites (through a stratified sample) is a rigorous and complex process. MOST of Us, or another expert in research design, can assist you in this process. Below are some general guidelines.

Your intervention area should:

☑ Hold a significant proportion of your target population

✓ Have measurable boundaries. You may want to limit your intervention area to one city, several counties or to a single Designated Market Area (a DMA is a radio or broadcast television coverage area)

✓ Be an area you can successfully saturate with your campaign messages, given your budget constraints

Your control area should:

✓ Hold a proportion of your target population similar to that of your intervention area

✓ Match your intervention area in terms of key socio-economic demographics and other key variables (dry or wet counties, rural or urban, etc.)

✓ Be non-contiguous with the intervention area. The two areas must be geographically separate so that campaign messages and publicity do not migrate from the intervention area into the control area. The sites should not be in neighboring counties, in the same Designated Market Area, or share radio or TV media outlets

Once you have selected matched sites, you should randomly assign them as intervention and control areas.

MOST of Us Tip: Downsize Reach to Increase Rigor

Implementing a small, controlled experiment can sometimes be a tough sell politically, since the intervention area will receive intensive program resources while other areas receive none. However, distributing resources equally may result in a diffuse, low-dosage campaign that would not achieve measurable results.

It is essential to convince your funding agency of the importance of carrying out a science-driven, controlled intervention that will show the efficacy and applicability of the model. Once a successful, controlled intervention has been completed, the program can be replicated in other areas.

STEP 1.6 CREATING YOUR PROGRAM TIMELINE

Setting a reasonable program timeline at the outset of your campaign will help you plan and staff your project, develop your budget, and make certain that you have allowed adequate time to meet your goals and objectives.

At the same time, you may want to set time limits or establish a schedule that dictates when to move on from one project element to the next. You could spend months on every intermediate step as you design and implement your campaign, but it is important not to get bogged down. Decide in advance how much time you want to spend on environmental advocacy, how much time refining your goals, how much time in focus groups. If you don't have a timeline that keeps your project moving forward, you may find yourself running out of momentum and resources before your work is done.

There are no hard and fast rules about how long it should take to plan and implement your campaign. In general, allow three to six months for planning and preparation. You should not expect to see significant results with an intervention of less than one year in duration. This does not mean that your ads have to be on television for 365 consecutive days; rather, your campaign must have a presence—sometimes more intense, sometimes less, sometimes on primetime television, sometimes on highway billboards—for at least this length of time. Be careful, however, not to spread your media out over such a long period that it dilutes your dosage.

» *See Appendix A for a sample six-month campaign snapshot.*

MOST of Us Tip: First Things First

It can be tempting to start work before you have a signed contract, especially if your funder is enthusiastic about your project. Hold out, for your sanity and theirs. Create a project timeline that begins the day the contract is signed, and resist the urge to begin preparations beforehand. Contracts can and do fall apart in the final hour.

STEP 1.7 *DEVELOPING A BUDGET*

Developing a budget is a complex process that depends upon many local variables, including your organization's available funding, the cost and competitiveness of the media market in your intervention area, and the size and salaries of your staff.

How much should I spend per person on media?

If we knew the answer to this question, we would be in Tahiti right now. The answer is a moving target, one that the big ad firms have spent millions of dollars trying to answer. There are no rules, except this: if you are running a high-intensity media campaign, media costs should make up a large percentage of your total budget.

During the 15-month MOST of Us Prevent Drinking and Driving Campaign, MOST of Us spent approximately $9 per person on media, including television, radio and newspaper advertisements, posters, billboards, theater slides, inside signs and promotional items.

At this cost, the campaign delivered its message at high dosages across an extremely large coverage area, and achieved strong message recognition. MOST of Us has also achieved statistically significant results in other campaigns at a fraction of this cost.

Montana is a relatively inexpensive and noncompetitive media market, where relatively few media outlets reach a large geographic area. Every media market will be different; you will want to consult or contract with a media or marketing specialist in your area. Wherever your intervention takes place, your per-person media costs will likely turn out to be less than the price of a headlight for your average SUV, and hundreds of dollars cheaper than the fines for getting pulled over for a DUI. For more on planning and buying media, see Steps 4 and 6.

SOCIAL NORMS SYNERGY

Synergy is when two or more forces interact so that their combined effect is greater than the sum of their individual effects. Social norms practitioners need to find ways to apply the social norms approach synergistically with other prevention strategies and efforts.

Opportunities for synergy are also opportunities to stretch your budget and create ways to disseminate your message. Look for other campaigns or prevention efforts that share your same goals, target audience, or intervention area. If you can "piggyback" your message onto these efforts, you can stretch your budget and benefit from the name recognition, trust and support other groups have already established.

Make sure, however, that any campaign you join forces with is compatible with the social norms approach. Traffic safety practitioners often employ as many strategies as possible and hope that one or some combination will prove effective. This is a "more is better" approach, which assumes that two or three strategies are better than one. However, different strategies (e.g. health terrorism and social norms) can compete and diminish each others' effectiveness if they are not compatible. A successful social norms strategy can work with and support law enforcement, policy change and other prevention measures, as long as they are administered together as part of a coordinated plan that takes advantage of their shared goals and strengths.

What if I don't have a big budget?

Unless you are Nike or Coca-Cola, you won't have the resources to reach the entire world. What is important is that your budget is appropriate for the target population or intervention area you are trying to reach. If you are stretched thin, narrow your target population or scale down your intervention area. If you run a program that is a mile wide and an inch deep, you will waste money and see no results. Use your data and research to refine your target to a concentrated or confined area. Make your money count.

There are also other, lower-cost ways to get your message out besides creating and placing your own media. It is possible to run a social norms campaign on a shoestring. Some creative options:

- Partner with an existing prevention campaign. Leverage your efforts, and infuse your social norms message into their existing work and materials.

- Work with local law enforcement. Educate them on the social norms approach, and find mutually beneficial ways to deliver the message.

- Create buzz through media advocacy, without spending a dime. Write op-eds, letters to the editor, and work with local reporters to get coverage of your issue from the social norms perspective.

- Approach your local university to find faculty, student and research help.

- Combine the social norms approach with other prevention strategies (see sidebar on "Social Norms Synergy").

MOST of Us Tip: Focus On Long-Term Results

Many projects are funded by annual grants. It can be difficult to plan when you don't know what your budget will be from one year to the next, or even if you will have funding at all. Since a campaign that is planned and executed in just 12 months is unlikely to produce measurable results or attract renewed funding, you may want to carry out the baseline survey and begin your media intervention with the hope that these efforts will attract the funding to continue your efforts for a second year.

» *See Appendix B for a campaign budget outline and worksheet.*

STEP 1.8 STAFFING

Project Leadership

The most essential decision for the success of your campaign is your selection of a project leader. The importance of good management cannot be underestimated. Even if your campaign message and materials are top-notch, your campaign will have little chance of success if you do not have a talented project leader to guide the campaign and manage its staff.

The skills and attitudes of a great social norms project leader include:

- ✓ A passion for the positive
- ✓ A commitment to achieving results
- ✓ The ability to work in a politically charged environment, on an issue about which people have strong opinions
- ✓ The instincts of a politician. A strong project leader should be comfortable having open, direct communication with high-level government officers, and be able to work alongside other people in the prevention community who may not support a social norms effort
- ✓ Rapid and confident decision-making skills
- ✓ Experience in community mobilization, coalition building and media relations
- ✓ The ability to educate and sell key stakeholders on the campaign goals and vision
- ✓ An understanding of the theory and application of social norms
- ✓ Experience as a leader—running a social norms intervention is not the best way to cut one's managerial teeth

In-House Staffing, Outsourcing and The Middle Path

During your campaign there will be projects you could assign to your in-house staff or outsource to an independent vendor. It is costly in both time and salaries to train and maintain a large staff to run your project. At the same time, you should not entrust your most important campaign elements to an outside group who may not understand the specific needs of a social norms campaign—especially when it comes to advertising.

MOST of Us has found that the best method is often somewhere in between, something we call "active brokering," where outsourced talent is managed as closely as if they were on your staff. By providing daily direction and guidance to your contractors, you can ensure that they are furthering the goals of your campaign.

» *The table on page 28 covers the pros and cons of different staffing options.*

STEP 1.9 *DOCUMENTING YOUR PROJECT*

Thoroughly document your project throughout its planning and implementation in a documents notebook. Record all of the steps you take to fulfill your project goals and objectives—including the obstacles you encounter along the way. Most importantly, record all of the coverage and feedback your campaign receives from the community and the media, as well as general coverage of driving after drinking in your intervention and control areas.

Your documents notebook will encompass a variety of printed, audio, and visual materials, including notes from focus groups and structured interviews, feedback from key stakeholders, newspaper articles from clipping services, op-eds, letters to the editor, comments written on posters, records of phone calls to your campaign office, and other input from the target population and the community as a whole.

This documentation serves to:

- ✓ Provide a clear history of events, efforts, and outcomes
- ✓ Facilitate any reporting (such as quarterly and year-end reports) your funder might require
- ✓ Make information readily available for colleagues, administrators, the media and others
- ✓ Provide access to and continuity of information in the event of staffing changes
- ✓ Assist in the evaluation of your project, both during its implementation and after its completion
- ✓ Help you monitor changes in the cultural context of driving after drinking
- ✓ Capture stories for press and news events
- ✓ Document the exact process of your intervention for evaluation and replication

Pros & Cons of Staffing Options

IN-HOUSE STAFFING	ACTIVE BROKERING	OUTSOURCING
PROS	**PROS**	**PROS**
higher level of control and more flexibility with timing	better quality of work	large pool of vendors to choose from
greater control over content and its production	easier to keep outsourced work in agreement with social norms theory	can hire a vendor on a job need basis
employee can be trained in social norms marketing	closer oversight of work in progress	not necessary to have equipment and space required for job
CONS	**CONS**	**CONS**
necessary to have employees with appropriate skills	high use of upper-level staff time	vendor may not be expert in social norms marketing
must have funding for position salary & benefits	need to allocate significant staff time to manage sub-contractors	more effort required to get the vendor to understand content needs
necessary to have equipment and space required for job		requires sticking to a strict timeline to meet deadlines

** *This table references Step 1.8 text on page 26*

The disparity between perceived norms and actual norms is what drives the social norms process. The collection of baseline data is when you first measure this disparity in your particular target audience. The survey data you collect will become the actual intervention tool that you will use to create change.

Misperceptions of Norms: The Hidden Risk Factor

Statistical analyses have shown that misperceptions of norms are one of the strongest predictors of high-risk behavior. However, in most studies this key risk factor remains hidden, because researchers do not ask the questions that would reveal it.

You've got to ask for it to get it. And that is precisely the purpose of your baseline survey: to capture this hidden risk factor by uncovering the ways in which your target audience overperceives risky behaviors and underperceives protective factors.

Collecting Social Norms Data

For a social norms campaign, you will need to collect information on the healthy attitudes and behaviors of your target population. This process requires much more than simply gathering data and flipping the statistics around to show their positive, majority side; uncovering this positive information requires a paradigm shift in how data is developed.

In a social norms campaign, data is not a tool for passing judgment. It is never used to prove how bad people are by focusing on how recklessly and ignorantly a few of them behave. To collect social norms data, you will need to cultivate the desire and ability to seek what is good and healthy in your target population. Your surveys must be specifically designed to uncover their most positive practices and values, and to pick up the most encouraging—rather than the most alarming—information and trends. Nevertheless, you will also want to measure harmful consequences and risks, so you can show if your campaign reduces them.

STEP 2.1 USING SELF-REPORTED DATA

There is no way to measure people's perceptions and attitudes except to ask about them directly. Since there is no measurement you can take or database you can access that will tell you what people think, social norms campaigns are reliant upon what is called "self-reported data." Self-reported data is used all of the time (think of the presidential and other opinion polls that are reported in the news every day). However, when you ask people about illegal behaviors, the reliability and validity of their responses can be called into question. To increase the reliability of your survey responses, make sure that your survey is confidential, anonymous, and voluntary—and ensure that your survey respondents know that these conditions are being met.

STEP 2.2 DESIGNING A SURVEY INSTRUMENT

The survey is the foundation of an effective social norms campaign. You will administer your survey in both the intervention and control areas at least twice during your campaign period. The results of the first survey will serve as your baseline data and become the basis of your social norms messages; the second and later surveys will track the impact of your campaign on your target population.

Designing an original survey is a difficult process, and you will most likely need an outside expert such as MOST of Us to do this work for you. The information in this chapter will allow to you work closely with your survey developers, and make sure they understand the requirements of social norms data collection.

MOST of Us Tip: Piggyback Surveys

There are many health and college surveys that include alcohol-related questions, such as the MOST of Us Youth Web Survey, the American College Health Assessment and the Southern Illinois University CORE Alcohol and Drug Survey, among others. In some cases it may be cost-effective to use one of these instruments and add your own perceptual questions to it.

The danger in relying on surveys that are not specifically designed for social norms is that their response categories are often not sensitive enough to measure even significant change. For example, say you have one survey response category for people who consume five to eight drinks before driving. Even if you run an extremely successful campaign that encourages heavier drinkers to reduce their number of drinks from eight to five, your follow-up surveys will not measure any change at all.

Your survey should collect data on your target population's attitudes, perceptions and behaviors regarding driving after drinking. Depending upon the goals of your campaign, you may also want to capture people's attitudes and perceptions about driving after drinking laws, regulations or enforcement policies. For example, during the MOST of Us

Prevent Drinking and Driving Campaign, MOST of Us collected information about support for passage of a .08% Blood Alcohol Content (BAC) legal limit for drivers in Montana. The results showed unanticipated support for the law among young adults in the intervention counties, a support that grew even stronger over the course of the campaign. MOST of Us presented these findings to the legislature in the hopes of influencing state policy; Montana later reduced the legal BAC for drivers to .08%.

A good survey should:

- ✓ Include questions about actual behavior
- ✓ Include questions about perceptions of peer behavior
- ✓ Include questions about individual values and attitudes
- ✓ Include questions about perceived peer values and attitudes
- ✓ Include questions about both descriptive norms (actual behavior) and injunctive norms (approval or disapproval of different behaviors)
- ✓ Include questions about message exposure (see "Exposure Testing," page 32)
- ✓ Acquire information on positive, protective factors (e.g., use of designated drivers or willingness to intervene to keep an impaired driver from getting behind the wheel)
- ✓ Include demographic questions (age, race, gender, educational background, area of residence)
- ✓ Include questions about height and weight to facilitate calculations of estimated Blood Alcohol Content
- ✓ Provide definitions for key terms (explain how many ounces of beer, wine or liquor constitutes one "drink")

SURVEY FATIGUE

While there are many elements your survey should contain, avoid the impulse to include everything under the sun. Your survey must be short enough so that people can take it without succumbing to "survey fatigue," which could cause them to abandon the survey mid-way, finish it inaccurately, or become annoyed with you and your campaign. Keep your survey as short and sweet as possible. Survey completion times should be roughly as follows:

WRITTEN SURVEY 15-20 minutes   **WEB SURVEY** 10-15 minutes   **PHONE SURVEY** 5-10 minutes

Descriptive vs. Injunctive Norms

There are two types of social norms: **descriptive norms** reflect how the majority behaves, while **injunctive norms** reflect majority attitudes. Your survey results might show that while only 40% of your target audience actually uses designated drivers (descriptive), 86% approves of or supports their use (injunctive). Even if your baseline data shows that most of your target group does not engage in the behavior you are trying to support, you can run a social norms campaign based upon the injunctive attitudes of the majority. You may want to include some injunctive messages in your campaign even if a majority does engage in the behavior you are trying to promote. People's values and opinions can be one of the most powerful ways to support change.

Exposure Testing

Exposure testing is the most direct and reliable way to measure if and how your message is being heard by your target audience. Questions about campaign exposure should be included in all of your surveys, including your baseline survey.

It is essential to obtain accurate figures on audience exposure because it is repeated, intense doses of the campaign message that leads to changes in perceptions and behavior. (See "How a Social Norms Campaign Works," page 11.) Use the results of your exposure testing to determine if changes to your media plan are necessary.

MOST of Us Tip: Exposure is Essential

If you do not get good results from your exposure testing, the rest of your survey results are meaningless. If you do not find high levels of campaign awareness, you cannot make the argument that your campaign is responsible for any of the changes in perceptions or behaviors that your surveys might reveal.

STEP 2.3 *FRAMING SURVEY QUESTIONS*

The quality of your survey questions determines the quality of the campaign messages you will be able to generate later. If you don't spend the time to carefully craft your survey questions, you may find yourself unable to generate useful messages from the resulting data. Whether you are writing your survey yourself or hiring someone to do it for you, it is important to be able to look critically at each question and understand the possible messages that could be generated from it.

The question is the message.

The simplest way to think about your survey questions is to look at them as actual

SAMPLE EXPOSURE TESTING QUESTIONS

1. During the past year, do you remember seeing or hearing any alcohol prevention campaign advertisements, posters, billboards or brochures?

2. What was the main message that you remember?

3. During the past year, how many times have you seen these advertisements on TV? (Ask about radio and all other advertising formats your campaign has employed.)

4. To what extent have these materials influenced your decision whether or not to drink and drive, ride with someone who has been drinking, or to drink excessively yourself?

campaign messages. As you write or review each survey question, flip it around to see what kind of message you might generate from it.

Question: Would you support or oppose changing the law in Montana to make a blood alcohol concentration above .08% constitute legal impairment?

Message: Most Montana young adults support changing the legal BAC limit for drivers to .08%.

Question: In the past 30 days, how often have you driven within one hour after drinking two or more alcoholic beverages?

Message: Most Montana young adults have not driven within one hour of drinking two or more alcoholic beverages in the past 30 days.

Each message should be accompanied by detailed information about the survey, as described in Step 3.3

Write questions that fail to be confusing in how they are worded.

In other words, clarity is key. There is a Saturday Night Live skit in which the boss at a nuclear reactor goes on vacation, leaving two idiot underlings in charge. His last words to them are: "Remember, you can't put too much water in a nuclear reactor." The two fight over whether this means that no amount of water is too much, or that too much could be a bad thing. Inevitably, they make the wrong choice, but the point is to make sure that your questions have only one possible interpretation. Take this question, for example:

"In the past year, have you found yourself in the position of deciding whether to ride in a car with a driver who had been drinking alcohol?"

If someone answers no, it could mean that they were not exposed to any potential impaired drivers, or that they drove with people who had been drinking multiple times, but never once considered not getting in the car.

Ask questions about positive and protective behaviors.

Surveys that focus solely on negative behaviors will not give you the information you need for a social norms campaign. You must also ask questions about the behaviors you hope to increase in order to uncover the majority information that supports them. Make sure to include questions about protective behaviors and actions, like using designated drivers or taking the keys away from an impaired friend.

Use reasonable and useful time frames.

Have-you-ever questions (like "Have you ever driven drunk?") are difficult to generate messages from and nearly impossible to use as evaluation tools. Many people may have done something once and never again; a question with an unlimited time frame does not capture actual, current behavior. It is best to ask questions with multiple time responses (e.g. never, yearly, monthly, weekly, daily). These will give more detailed resolution to your survey results, and provide you with various options for creating messages.

Take this question and its answer stem, for example:

> **In the past 12 months, how often have you driven a car or other vehicle while drinking alcohol or after drinking alcohol?**
>
> | | |
> |---|---|
> | a. **Never** | d. **Twice a month** |
> | b. **Once a year** | e. **Once a week** |
> | c. **Once a month** | f. **Twice or more a week** |

If the results show that only 65% of your target audience regularly uses designated drivers in the typical month, you can look to your weekly numbers to see if they show a stronger norm.

Another way to frame your questions is to ask what is most typical (e.g., "When you drink, do you typically have a non-drinking designated driver?"). These questions quickly capture the normative frame, and are great for messaging. You can also ask what people did the last time they were in a given situation (e.g., "The last time you were out drinking, did you have a non-drinking designated driver?"). It is sometimes easier for people to recall what they did "last time" than to estimate what is most typical of them.

» *See Appendix C for a sample social norms survey.*

MOST of Us Tip: Test Perceptions of Statistics

61%... 56%... 52%... When does a norm become too weak to be an effective tool for correcting misperceptions? The best way to find out is to ask your audience. Different audiences—college students versus law enforcement officers, for example— will have different reactions to the same norms, depending upon their issue tolerance. Focus-group your statistics to see how they are perceived. Your audience will tell you what they think constitutes a strong majority.

STEP 2.4 SELECTING YOUR SAMPLING FRAME

You can administer your survey online or by phone, mail, or e-mail. In-person survey administration and point-intercept interviews are also options, but these types of surveys are expensive and logistically difficult to carry out.

You will need experts in survey administration to help you choose the right sampling frame for your project. The information below will help you ask the right questions of the people who will administer your survey.

Web Survey

PROS	CONS
Good for reaching community audiences	
Relatively inexpensive	Requires technical support and expertise
Comfortable for respondents, increased feeling of anonymity	Potential for low response rate
Data automatically entered into computer system for instant retrieval	
The MOST of Us survey system has specific programming protocols that make it completely anonymous and confidential	Not all web surveys are set up to offer complete anonymity to respondents

To try out the MOST of Us web survey and online survey platform, visit **mostofus.org**.

MOST of Us Tip: MOST of Us Surveys and Technology

MOST of Us has created several brief, reliable and accurate social norms survey instruments that can be administered by web, phone or using scannable paper forms. We can add additional questions to one of these surveys, or create custom surveys precisely for your campaign. MOST of Us has also designed a cutting-edge online survey system. This platform is an innovative, low-cost way to reach large numbers of people and achieve quick and accurate results with any survey.

Phone Survey

PROS	CONS
Good for reaching community audiences	
Once contracted, little staff oversight necessary	Extremely expensive
Call center can keep trying numbers until the survey sample is filled	Can be difficult to get working numbers for members of target audience
Easy to reach the desired number of respondents in each demographic category	May exclude cell phone users
	Can take a month to receive data

» *See Appendix D for sample Phone Survey Specifications.*

Mail Survey

PROS	CONS
Less expensive than phone survey	Labor-intensive to administer
	Requires more work from respondents, which may discourage participation
	Low response rates
	Takes 4–8 weeks to tally and analyze data

E-mail Survey

PROS	CONS
Relatively inexpensive	Email may be seen as "spam"
Easy for respondents to fill out	Potential for low response rate
	No anonymity for respondents

Sample Size

The sample size (or "n") of a survey depends on many variables—including what you plan to do with your data. You will need to consult with MOST of Us or another survey administration expert to help you determine the ideal sample size for your specific target population, sampling frame, budget, and project goals.

STEP 2.5 *CREATING YOUR DATA COLLECTION SCHEDULE*

You will need to administer a minimum of two surveys: a baseline survey and at least one follow-up. If your budget allows, you may want to schedule one or two intermediate surveys to track the changes in your intervention area as they happen. Your final follow-up survey should be scheduled shortly after the conclusion of your campaign.

Do not schedule any survey within 30 days after a holiday or event that is usually associated with heavy drinking. Avoid local happenings and festivals that encourage drinking, and any holidays that might draw a large portion of your target population away from their home areas.

TIMING MATTERS

You will get very different results if you ask about drinking behaviors on New Year's Day than if you ask in the middle of August. Think about when you are scheduling your survey, and how that timing might skew your results.

Holidays and Events to Avoid:

New Year's Eve	Spring Break	Labor Day
Superbowl	Memorial Day	Halloween
St. Patrick's Day	July 4th	Homecoming

STEP 2.6 *SURVEY ADMINISTRATION*

If you do not have the staff or resources to conduct the survey yourself, never fear, you can outsource. Believe it or not, people do this for a living, and actually like it. Contract with MOST of Us, or solicit bids from several research firms or universities. Make sure to give each vendor the same specifications, including:

- ✓ Type of administration (phone, mall, etc.)
- ✓ Time frame for survey administration
- ✓ Deadline for survey completion and data reporting
- ✓ Required number of completed surveys
- ✓ Requirements for sample demographics
- ✓ Requirements for control vs. treatment samples, if applicable
- ✓ Format in which you want to receive the data

Make sure you double- and triple-check any survey for accuracy before you send it out to be administered.

STEP 2.7 *STATISTICAL ANALYSIS*

Unless you have a statistician on staff, you will want to contract with MOST of Us or another research firm or university to administer your survey and to analyze the resulting data.

Think about how you want your data broken down: you may want detailed comparisons of the responses of men versus women, drinkers versus non-drinkers, or of the norms for different minorities or age groups. The basic descriptive statistics are fairly simple to compute. However, you should make sure that whoever does your original calculations lays the groundwork for sophisticated post-test analyses such as factor and regression analysis.

STEP 2.8 *TRIANGULATING FROM OTHER SOURCES OF DATA*

Much in the same way that it takes several compass readings to calculate your exact location on a map, multiple sources and types of data can be used to provide a more complete picture of your target population's relationship to driving after drinking. This process of using a variety of measures to create a more accurate picture of the data is called **triangulation**.

Sources of measurable and objective data include:

- Fatal Analysis Reporting System (FARS)
- State Department of Transportation crash statistics
- Other state-collected data
- ER reports
- Arrest convictions
- DUI/DWI and BAC data

Sources of qualitative or anecdotal data include:

- Focus groups
- Structured interviews
- Artifacts
- Documents

The process of triangulation is a complex one, requiring significant expertise. You will likely need help from MOST of Us or another outside group to derive meaningful, relevant information from these sources of data.

Message development is a rigorous process that involves deriving stories and statistics from your baseline data. The scope of your message is determined by your target population's readiness for change, their current norms and their normative perceptions.

STEP 3.1 *PRINCIPLES OF SOCIAL NORMS MESSAGES*

Your campaign messages should be designed to correct the misperceptions about driving after drinking identified by your baseline survey. To align with the principles of social norms theory, these messages should be:

Positive. Your messages should promote what is good and healthy in your target group.

Normative. Technically, a normative statistic is anything over 50%. However, people in your community are unlikely to be happy if you tell them that 51% of their peers do not drive drunk. Remember that some norms are stronger than others; use your best numbers in your messages.

Reflective. Mirror your target population's best behavior back to them in a way that is designed to change misperceptions. Avoid being prescriptive, preachy or autocratic.

Inclusive. Create messages that speak to the diversity of your target population.

Neutral. State statistics and facts in a nonjudgmental tone. To embrace good statistics too positively can create the impression that you do not see a need for further change. Even if 90% of the people in your target population do not drive while impaired, that number can be improved upon.

Clear. Keep your messages as simple and straightforward as possible.

Data-based and source-specific. Truthfulness and accuracy are central to your campaign. The data source should be an integral part of every message—not fine print at the bottom of the page.

Develop Multiple Messages
Although the MOST of Us Prevent Drinking and Driving intervention achieved statistically significant results with a single campaign message, the single-message approach has limitations and does not reflect state-of-the-art practice in the social norms field.

A single message is highly vulnerable to criticism, and can even erode your campaign's credibility if it is heard as a slogan rather than as an accurate reflection of true norms. By using multiple messages, you can better address the complexity of driving after drinking and the sophistication of your target audience.

You may want to generate messages on different norms revealed by your data (such as designated driver use or other protective factors) or communicate directly with different segments of your target audience. You may decide to address men and women individually, or to create messages tailored to certain age groups, or to people who are part of specific communities within your intervention area. Each message should be placed so that it will reach its desired audience.

Core Values and Data-Based Messages

Before you begin generating messages from your baseline data, it is essential to identify

---

IDENTIFY THE SOCIAL NORMS MESSAGES

Thinking in terms of social norms theory can be counterintuitive at first, since we are so trained to frame issues in terms of problems, danger and risk. Be vigilant: make sure that consequence-based, aversive thinking does not seep into your campaign materials. Below is a quick exercise to help you learn to recognize strong social norms messages.

	YES	NO
a. Most San Diego Teens (85%) Won't Ride with an Impaired Driver	_____	_____
b. One out of Three Ohio Young Adults Doesn't Drink and Drive	_____	_____
c. 86% Could Have Died, But Chose Not to Drink and Drive	_____	_____
d. 46% of Kentucky Young Adults Don't Drink and Drive	_____	_____
e. Dare to Be Different: Use a Designated Driver	_____	_____
f. Help Us Transform the Norm: Don't Drink and Drive	_____	_____
g. 96% of Montana Adults Support Stricter Law Enforcement to Combat Driving After Drinking	_____	_____
h. Stop Drinking and Driving. Today.	_____	_____

Answers: **a.** Yes **b.** No, not normative **c.** No, includes negative, fear-based elements **d.** No, not normative **e.** No, implies it is not normative to use a designated driver **f.** No, implies it is normative to drink and drive **g.** Yes **h.** No, includes a command on how to behave.

MOST of Us Tip: It's All About the Messages

Message development actually begins long before you get the results of your survey. If you don't choose a campaign goal that can be achieved by correcting misperceptions, don't word your survey questions thoughtfully or don't create sensitive response categories, you are going to find yourself with limited options when it comes to message development. Take the time to plan ahead.

the core value of your campaign. The core value is your campaign's central belief or tenet, such as "We all deserve safe roads free of impaired drivers." Your core value should capture the positive spirit of the campaign.

Your core value should be a point of consensus agreement. Every prevention specialist, law enforcement officer, politician and community member should be able to agree with the core value of your campaign. The core value also becomes a platform from which to develop messages. Grounding your data-based messages in this core value will help ensure that audiences do not misperceive the meaning of your messages or the intent behind them.

When you separate your statistical messages from your core value, it becomes possible for some people to read your messages as advertisements for complacency (e.g. "4 out of 5 Don't Drink and Drive and that's good enough") rather than a means of reinforcing and promoting positive community values. By reminding your audience of the core value regularly, you provide the proper context in which your messages should be interpreted.

STEP 3.2 DEVELOPING YOUR SOCIAL NORMS MESSAGES

The messages you create should be designed to correct misperceptions and aligned with the specific goals you set at the outset of your campaign.

Examine your baseline survey. Look for pairings of results which show that a majority *does not* engage in a risky behavior, while a strong majority *believes that most people do.* For example, the baseline survey for the MOST of Us Prevent Drinking and Driving Campaign showed that while 79.6% of Montana young adults had not driven drunk in the previous month, 92% believed that the average young adult had.

Choose several results that mesh with your campaign goals, and develop a number of data-based messages from each, making sure they are positive, normative, reflective, neutral, clear, and source-specific. Try different wordings and phrases, and vary the ways

MOST of Us Tip: Increase Protection and Reduce Risk

Most people overestimate the prevalence of risky behaviors; at the same time, they underestimate the frequency of positive, protective behaviors. You should create messages designed to correct both types of misperceptions: tell your audience that most of them do not drive after drinking, and that most of them do use designated drivers or take the keys away from a friend who has been drinking.

in which you present the statistical results (e.g. 75% vs. 3 out of 4). These are the preliminary messages that you will test with your target audience and key stakeholders.

Your preliminary messages should:

- ✓ Capture the spirit of consensus
- ✓ Convey that the majority of your target population practices healthy, protective behaviors or is supportive of healthy, protective behaviors
- ✓ Be consistent with your program goal
- ✓ Portray the desired goal (e.g. use of designated drivers) as a socially acceptable choice
- ✓ Be credible to your target group
- ✓ Include accurate statistics from your baseline survey
- ✓ Employ facts, not just slogans, tag lines or catchy phrases
- ✓ Be careful not to imply tacit approval of illegal or problem behaviors
- ✓ Focus on the positive
- ✓ Frame the seriousness of—and avoid minimizing—the problem

Think carefully about how your messages should be framed. Try to align or "package" them with the core values or identity of your target group (e.g., control, independence, spontaneity, fairness).

Of course you will want to create most vivid and memorable message possible, but don't set your heart on creating a slogan that is as snappy as "Coke Is It" or "Just Do It." There is simply too much essential context and information that you must provide. It is meaningless to have your audience hear and remember your message if they don't understand it in a way that corrects their misperceptions.

MOST of Us Tip: Find the Energy of Dissonance

Remember that social norms is a data-driven process. If your data uncovers an issue that has unexpectedly dramatic misperceptions attached to it, you may want to create messages to address it. After all, the element of the driving after drinking issue that members of your target group perceive most inaccurately is the one that has the greatest potential for change.

STEP 3.3 CONTEXTUALIZE MESSAGES

Your message must be supported by all of the relevant details about the data, such as:

- ✓ The age range of the respondents
- ✓ The response rate
- ✓ The quantity of alcohol that defines a "drink"
- ✓ The time frame to which the data refers
- ✓ The name of the sponsoring agency

This information should appear on your posters and printed materials, and should be included, whenever possible, in your radio and television ads. Context is essential if you want your message to be credible to your audience, and received as positive information.

MOST of Us Tip: Oops! Learn from Our Mistakes

In an effort to create a short, memorable slogan, the central message in the MOST of Us Prevent Drinking and Driving Campaign was pared down to "MOST of Us (4 out of 5) Don't Drink and Drive." However, because we did not adequately qualify the numbers—by grounding them in a core value or explaining that they referred to the behavior of 21- to 34-year olds who had been drinking in the previous 30 days—the message created the impression that, at any given moment, 1 out of every 5 cars on the road was being driven by an impaired driver, which was certainly not the case.

STEP 3.4 INJUNCTIVE VS. DESCRIPTIVE SOCIAL NORMS MESSAGES

Once again, there are two types of social norms: descriptive norms reflect how the majority behaves, while injunctive norms reflect their attitudes. Injunctive norms messages can be less controversial than ones based on descriptive norms. In addition, a strong injunctive norm can help strengthen a weaker descriptive norm. For example, the fact that 97% of Montanans support stricter laws to prevent driving after drinking (injunctive) supports the message that 80% of Montana young adults don't drink and drive (descriptive). The most effective campaigns will mix both types of messages.

DESCRIPTIVE VS. INJUNCTIVE SOCIAL NORMS QUESTIONS AND MESSAGES

Descriptive Question: During the past 12 months, have you driven within one hour after you have consumed two or more alcoholic beverages?

Message: Most Montana young adults (4 out of 5) don't drive within one hour after having two or more drinks.

Injunctive Question: Would you support or oppose changing the law in Montana to make a BAC above .08% constitute legal impairment?

Message: Most Montana Young Adults support strengthening state BAC laws to .08%.

The Seriousness of Driving after Drinking ≠ The Prevalence of the Behavior

It is critical to separate the seriousness of driving after drinking from its prevalence when you construct your media messages. The minority that engages in driving after drinking presents a serious threat to us all. A message that stresses the seriousness of the problem without making clear that it is deviant, minority behavior can easily support exaggerated misperceptions about the frequency and acceptability of driving after drinking.

EXAMPLE DRIVING AFTER DRINKING MESSAGES

- Most Montana young adults (4 out of 5) don't drive within one hour after having two or more drinks.

- The Mile High City sets the limit: 78% of Denver's young adults support a .08% BAC legal alcohol limit for drivers.

- 3 out of 4 18- to 24-year-olds in Southern Ohio use sober designated drivers in a typical night out.

Audience Segmentation and Message Salience

How do you accurately make the distinction between the attitudes and behaviors of the majority and the actions of those whose beliefs or practices lie outside this overwhelming norm?

The answer lies in segmenting your audience into different target sub-groups and creating messages specifically tailored to each one. In a regional or statewide intervention, it may be impossible to create one message that will appeal to the diversity of your target audience. Finding salient messages that are appropriate for and relevant to different sub-groups may be essential to the success of your campaign.

Take care, however, not to single out a particular population in a way that brands its members as being particularly unhealthy or prone to dangerous behavior. Doing so would reinforce the negative identity of the group and work against your campaign aims. Keep all of your messages positive and encouraging.

It is also important that these tailored messages do not define your targeted subgroups more narrowly than they define themselves. For example, social norms programs on some college campuses have surveyed first-year students and then run campaigns based on their norms. This strategy is flawed, however, since incoming students don't look only to each other for behavioral direction, but also at the norms of the campus population at large.

MOST of Us Tip: Consider All Audiences

Remember that your campaign will not only be seen by your target audience, but also by the larger community of which they are a part, as well as the key stakeholders in your issue and campaign. A successful social norms campaign will create messages and materials that appeal to their shared values, goals and understanding.

STEP 3.5 *DEVELOPING A VISUAL DESIGN*

Once you have selected your preliminary messages, you need to develop the most appealing way to deliver them to your target audience.

Start with a poster. Posters are a relatively simple and inexpensive format in which to develop visual looks and test your messages. Poster designs can later be reused for brochures, billboards, and promotional items.

Before you begin, you and your graphic designer should look at materials from effective social norms efforts. Don't remake mistakes that have generously been made for you by others. Also look at movies, magazines and books directed towards your target group. Advertisers spend millions of dollars studying what colors, images, or other attributes their targets find appealing. You can learn from their research.

Creating and Choosing Images

We strongly recommend that you purchase stock images from a photo library instead of hiring a photographer to create original photographs. Stock images give you access to hundreds of images for only a few hundred dollars, while costs for a single photo shoot can run up to $1500 or more. Of course, images of local places and landmarks (such as a student union building on a college campus or a county courthouse) can reinforce the relevance of your campaign for your audience.

MOST of Us Tip: Independently Test Messages and Images

In your focus groups and pilot tests, test your images and messages separately, then bring the two together in the strongest combination you find. This will prevent a "bad" image from bringing a good message down (or vice versa) and make sure that you end up with the best possible result.

Online image banks are great sources for photographs and images. The purchase of "royalty free" images allows nearly unlimited lifetime use in any medium. Image CDs offer a large number of images for a low cost ($500–$700 for 30–100 images). Review all user agreements for specific information about reproduction and usage.

If you do decide to create original images, make sure you have a very specific concept before you begin, one that you have confirmed through pretesting will be appealing to your target group. You do not want to hire a photographer, find models, scout a location, and spend hours of staff time arranging and overseeing a shoot only to end up with images you cannot use.

Whichever method you choose, make sure you have a contract with the stock library or releases from photographers and models that grant you lifetime rights to the images.

》 *See Appendix E for a sample Talent Release Form.*

Your images should:

✓ Include minorities and other sub-populations

✓ Show models that look the age of the target audience, and none that look younger than 21

✓ Look natural and unstaged

✓ Avoid recognizable locations unless your campaign area is very small

✓ Omit visible logos on models' clothing or in background

✓ Not depict or glamorize harmful behavior

✓ Be appropriate to the season (avoid snow skiing images in summer)

✓ Be appropriate for the geographical region (avoid snow skiing photos in Florida)

✓ Show models wearing appropriate safety equipment (helmets on bikers, seatbelts on people in cars)

Graphic Design

Ask your graphic designer to create three or four pilot designs using your preliminary messages and your selected images. Remember that the message (and its survey-based statistic) should be the central focus of every ad. You do not want to choose an arresting image and have the normative message hidden at the bottom of the page.

TIPS FOR WORKING WITH GRAPHIC DESIGNERS

STYLE. Review potential designers' portfolios. Make sure their style is appropriate for your campaign.

RATE. Decide at the outset whether you want to pay an hourly rate or a job rate. If you are using a job rate, be aware of how many revisions you are allowed for that flat fee. An hourly rate is usually better for simpler jobs (putting a message on a pencil, for example) while a job rate is preferable for complex projects that might require a lot of input and refining (creating a brochure or billboard).

CHANGES. Negotiate how many changes you can ask for without getting charged. You will need leeway to make a significant number of changes in the first few draft designs.

DEADLINES. Set firm deadlines, and make sure they are specified in the contract.

STICK TO SOCIAL NORMS STYLE. Show potential designers material from other social norms campaigns to give them an idea of what the end product should look like. Give your chosen designer a clear list of "dos and don'ts" related specifically to social norms and your campaign. Your designer may object, and claim that he is an "advertising expert" or an "artist" and thus knows best. Remind him that a social norms campaign is a scientific study that must adhere to certain principles.

Your poster must include:

1 Your normative message

2 A credible data source

3 An engaging photo

4 Your website address

5 A disclaimer (such as "Any amount of alcohol may be illegal or dangerous") if you are targeting drivers below the legal drinking age

6 Statistics from your survey

7 A recognizable campaign logo

8 Your funder's name or logo

What does this poster lack? Only a few of the most essential ingredients for credible social norms messaging, including:

- The definition of a drink (i.e., how many ounces of beer, wine or hard alcohol equals one drink)

- The definition of driving after drinking (e.g., more than 2 drinks within one hour of getting behind the wheel, calculated BAC or another definition)

- The age range of the respondents (e.g., 21- to 34-year-old Montanans)

- The survey time frame (e.g., within the past 30 days)

- The sample size (e.g., n=1000)

MOST of Us Tip: Think Upper Left

As a rule of thumb, the upper left section of the page (and the writing in the largest text) are the most attention-getting. The central message should "pop" immediately off the page.

The creation of a marketing plan begins by seeing things through the eyes of your target population. Traditional and non-traditional media approaches are assessed for their potential to reach the desired audience. The results of these assessments are incorporated into a campaign-specific plan.

STEP 4.1 DEVELOP AN ADVERTISING AND MARKETING PLAN

A well-designed advertising and marketing plan will sustain the exposure of your campaign for the time and intensity necessary to create a shift in your target audience's perceptions. A high level of exposure is accomplished by maximizing the reach (the percentage of the target population that sees your message), the frequency (the average number of times each target individual is exposed to your message), and the duration of the campaign.

As you begin to design your plan, remember that social norms marketing is much more than a series of commercials, posters, and promotional items. It is about starting and steering a conversation—not one *between* you and your target audience, but one *among* your target audience. Effective social norms campaigns do not have an authoritarian or autocratic tone. Your job is to *rub people the wrong way with the right data*, and to get them talking among themselves.

Once your campaign launches, your audience and the community at large will talk about it. They will love, hate, disbelieve and question your message, and the volume of their dialogue (even if it is a critical one) will be a measure of your success. Your market plan will initiate and steer this powerful, perception-changing conversation. By getting people talking—and by giving them, through your messages, a different story to tell among themselves about who they are when it comes to driving after drinking—your market plan turns your target audience into its own engine of change.

STEP 4.2 PLANNING ADVERTISING

Your target audience is more likely to remember and be engaged by a varied advertising campaign than by a single, endlessly-repeated ad. You will need to create multiple ads and roll them out in a series of media "flights."

- Each new advertisement should build upon previous ones. Vary the phrasing, visuals, characters and stories represented in each, and make sure to incorporate feedback from earlier testing.

- The number of ads you develop depends on the population of your intervention area. The greater the population, and the denser and more competitive the media environment, the more ads you will need to create in order to be noticed and remembered.

- Rotate the ads that are in play, and do not keep any single radio or television spot on air for longer than two months at a time. It is better to retire an ad and bring it back after a break.

Sample Media Grid for Year-Long High-Intensity Media Intervention

	JAN	FEB	MAR	APR	MAY	JUN	JUL	AUG	SEP	OCT	NOV	DEC
TV-PAID	▨	▨	▨			▨		▨		▨	▨	▨
RADIO-PAID	▨	▨	▨			▨				▨	▨	▨
TV-PSA				▨	▨	▨						
RADIO-PSA								▨	▨			
COLLEGE PAPER			▨							▨		
LOCAL NEWSPAPERS					▨						▨	
PROMOTIONAL ITEMS	▨	▨	▨				▨	▨	▨			
THEATER SLIDES	▨	▨	▨	▨	▨	▨	▨	▨	▨	▨	▨	▨
BILLBOARDS	▨				▨		▨		▨	▨		▨

Other possible paid advertising venues include:

- Community newspapers
- Milk cartons
- Public transportation ad space
- "Crawler" on the Weather Channel
- Flyers or mats for food trays in fast-food chains

MOST of Us Tip: Localize Your Market Plan

The best advertising and marketing plan for one intervention area may not be the best for another. Each plan should be culturally specific and unique to the place where the intervention will take place. Consult with local media and marketing experts for advice on how to run a campaign in your area.

STEP 4.3 *BUYING MEDIA*

It is relatively easy to purchase newspaper ads, billboards, and movie theater slides. Your organization can make these placements in-house. Purchasing television and radio ads, on the other hand, is a complex process. You will need an advertising or marketing firm to plan and place this type of media for you.

PAID VS. FREE MEDIA

MOST of Us has run campaigns using both paid and free media, and has found that using paid media is a far more effective means of delivering the social norms message. Paid media allows you place advertising at the precise times, places and venues where your target audience will be exposed to it. Donated television and radio airtime simply cannot reach the target audience with the precision and frequency required to effect change. And unlike news articles and other free media coverage of your campaign, using paid media guarantees that your message will reach your target audience in the exact words and format you choose.

Media Buys

Before you contract with a firm, ask several to give you detailed media buys—plans that outline the placement and cost of your campaign advertising—that are tailored to your target audience and conform to your budget. Compare the media buys to determine which firm is thinking most strategically about your campaign goals and needs. Be wary of agencies that place media without enough planning; the reach, frequency and cost-effectiveness of each media option must be taken into consideration.

Bonus Buys

If you work for a nonprofit or government entity, most media outlets will grant you "bonus buys," free media space in addition to your paid time. Ask potential media placement agencies how they plan to negotiate for bonus buys, and review their media plans to see how many bonus buys they have included. The upside of bonus buys is, of course, free ad time. The downside is that you have no control over when they run. They will usually be placed in whatever open spots are available, and will often be bumped in favor of paid ads.

Remember that bonus buys are a standard offering from most media outlets. Your marketing or advertising company will brag that it was their hard bargaining and insider connections that won you free media. Don't be fooled! Receiving as much as an additional 50% to 100% of your media free is often standard in the business.

MOST of Us Tip: Plan Ahead for Contracts

If you work for a state-funded agency, you will likely have to to solicit bids from media placement firms with a Request for Proposals (RFP). Make sure to budget ample time for this involved and time-consuming process. It can take up to a month to draft your RFP, and it is customary to keep the bidding period open for a month.

When putting your media buy (or any other contract) out for bid, include a renewal clause that will allow extension of the contract by one, two, or as many years as your agency allows, depending upon how much work you think you might want from the company in the future. This will allow you to renew your contract without repeating the lengthy RFP process, and can also allow you to negotiate a lower commission rate from your media placement firm. A firm that might charge you a 10% commission for one year's work may charge only 7 or 8% on the possibility of a multi-year project.

Post-Buy Reports

Post-buy reports outline the weekly, monthly and total Gross Rating Points (GRPs) for any given media flight. Post-buy reports need to be clearly written and easily read and understood by someone who is not a media expert, such as your project funder. Ask each bidding media firm for a sample post-buy report, and make the timely delivery of post-buys a requirement of your contract.

The post-buy analysis that your media placement company will provide will likely paint an extremely optimistic picture of audience exposure—one, frankly, that is not entirely reliable. Conducting your own exposure research is the only way to accurately determine how much your message is being heard and remembered by your target population. (See "Exposure Testing," page 32.)

MOST of Us Tip: Data is Power

Even though you will require detailed post-buys from your media firm, keep your own records of which ads you place in which markets during which periods. Documenting your media as you go will save you time and heartache later when you try to report on and evaluate your campaign.

HOW TO SOUND LIKE A MEDIA PRO

ART PROOF: Artwork for an ad, as submitted for client approval.

AUDIENCE: The number of people or households exposed to an ad, without regard to whether they actually saw or heard the material conveyed by that ad.

AUDIENCE DUPLICATION: The number of people who saw or heard more than one of the programs or publications in which an ad was placed.

AVERAGE AUDIENCE: The number of homes or persons tuned to a television program during an average minute, or the number of persons who viewed an average issue of a print publication.

BONUS BUY: Free media space given to non-profit or governmental organizations.

CAMERA-READY ART: Artwork that is ready to be photographed for printing.

CIRCULATION: For a print publication, the average number of copies distributed. For outdoor advertising this refers to the total number of people who have an opportunity to observe a billboard or poster. This term sometimes is used for broadcast, as well, but the term "audience" is used more frequently.

DESIGNATED MARKET AREA (DMA): A geographic designation that specifies which counties fall into a specific television market.

DOSAGE: The product of reach and frequency, expressed in Gross Rating Points (GRPs).

EARNED MEDIA: Positive, free media coverage that an organization must often work to generate, such as an op-ed or news story.

EARNED RATE: A discounted media rate, based on volume or frequency of media placement.

EXPOSURE: Consumers who have seen (or heard) a media vehicle, whether or not they paid attention to it.

FLIGHTING: A media schedule that involves more advertising at certain times and less advertising during other time periods.

FOCUS GROUP: A research method that brings together a small group of consumers to discuss a product or advertising, under the guidance of a trained interviewer.

FREQUENCY: Number of times an average person or home is exposed to a media vehicle (or group of vehicles), within a given time period.

Continued on following page

HOW TO SOUND LIKE A MEDIA PRO (CONTINUED)

GROSS AUDIENCE: The combined audiences for all media in a campaign. Some or much of the gross audience may actually represent duplicated audience.

GROSS IMPRESSIONS: Total number of unduplicated people or households represented by a given media schedule.

GROSS RATING POINTS (GRPs): Reach times average frequency. This is a measure of the advertising weight delivered by an ad or campaign within a given time period.

LOCAL RATE: An advertising rate charged to a local advertiser by local media and publications, as distinguished from a national rate that is charged to a national advertiser.

MEDIA PLAN: An advertising plan designed to reach a target demographic through media timing and selection.

PUBLIC SERVICE ANNOUNCEMENT (PSA): A commercial on television or radio that serves the public interest and is run by the media at no charge.

RATE CARD: Information cards, provided by both print and broadcast media, which contain information concerning advertising costs, mechanical requirements, issue dates, closing dates, cancellation dates, and circulation data.

RATING POINT: In television, the percentage of all TV households who are viewing a particular station at a given time. In radio, the percentage of all listeners who are listening to a particular station at a given time. Both instances vary depending on time of day.

REACH: The estimated number of individuals in the audience of a broadcast that is reached at least once during a specific period of time.

TARGET RATING POINTS (TRPs): GRPs adjusted to represent target demographic dosage.

Adapted from The University of Texas at Austin Department of Advertising website, http://advertising.utexas.edu/research/terms

STEP 4.4 EVALUATING MEDIA BUYS

Here are some important tips on television and radio advertising which will help you analyze proposed media buys and discuss placement options with your media firm.

- **Cheaper is not always better.** It can be cost-effective to pay for ads during times and programs that you know are popular with your target audience. Some media buyers will assume that you want to buy cheap spots, even if these time slots earn little or no audience. Depending upon your target audience, you may be better off buying a few ads on *Monday Night Football* than buying 50 midnight ads on obscure cable stations.

- **Make sure you are reaching your target population.** Look for clues that a media buy is not well planned. For example, if you are trying to keep 21- to 34-year-olds from driving after drinking, you should not buy radio time early on Saturday or Sunday mornings. People who are likely to drink and drive are probably not up at 6:00 am on the weekends.

- **Cable TV has different coverage areas than broadcast.** Different towns in the same area may receive different cable channels. Make sure that your entire target area receives the stations on which you advertise. Also, cable can have larger market areas than broadcast stations, so make sure cable ads will not run in your control area.

- **Cable ads are cheaper than broadcast ads.** Cable stations tend to place the ads on what they call "Run of Schedule" (ROS), which means wherever they have available space. You can place ads on specific cable shows for a higher price.

- **Cable buys usually come in "packages" of channels.** Make sure the majority of the channels in a cable package appeal to your target audience.

- **Cable viewers tend to watch broadcast TV in primetime and cable in the off-hours.** Buy your media accordingly.

- **When buying broadcast TV, avoid ROS except during the summer.** During the prime broadcast season from fall to spring, buying ROS can mean that your ads will air on shows that have few or no viewers.

PROMOTIONAL ITEMS

Promotional items have gone in and out of favor. They have often been misused as a branding tool for funding agencies or as a way to disseminate "health terrorist" messages. As a result, they have come to be seen as ineffective, and your funders may balk at having their money used to purchase keychains, tee shirts and other items. MOST of Us has found promotional items to be an important component of its campaigns.

Promotional items can be a great way to disseminate your campaign messages. They help grab people's attention, create goodwill (everyone loves free stuff!) and build momentum and buzz for your campaign. Promotional items work best as part of a larger marketing strategy.

Some tips for radio placement:

- **Buying "drive time" (6–10 am and 2–6 pm) on radio is expensive.** Nevertheless, it is often worth the price, since drive time is when the greatest number of people are tuned in.

- **Buy at least 5 spots a day on radio.** The majority of radio ads are ROS. If you buy fewer than five spots per day, your ad will run too infrequently to be noticed. Ten ads per day is often ideal, placed in a combination of ROS and drive-time spots.

STEP 4.5 PLANNING MARKETING

Marketing can help you increase your target audience's exposure to your campaign message through means other than advertising. There are many ways to reach your target group; each should be assessed for its effectiveness, credibility, and potential to generate exposure.

Think creatively about your target population and the places they spend their time. Are there stores, taverns, roads, social events, movie theaters or clinics where you could deliver your message to them? Creative ways to get your message out include:

Reach Out to the Public

- Perform interviews on television and radio programs. Share your campaign message and make news about the positive social norms approach.

- Have a charismatic person from your campaign present your message to local service, law enforcement, civic, church, and substance abuse prevention groups.

- Look for and take advantage of public speaking opportunities.

Partner with Other Groups

- Create a petition in support of the campaign and message.

- Organize a letter-writing campaign to the editor of the local paper.

- Put ads in the paper with the signatures of community members, groups and businesses who support your campaign.

- Seek sponsorship of state or national associations.

- Involve the United Way, YWCA, or Salvation Army.

- Involve other organizations with goals similar to your own.

Work with Local Businesses

- Partner with a pizza company to place a flyer or stamp on delivery boxes.
- Negotiate with local bottling companies to put your message on beverage containers.
- Ask car dealerships to mention your message in their ads.
- Work with Tavern Associations to place posters or coasters in bars and restaurants.
- Place the message on grocery bags and in laundromats, coffee shops, banks, gas stations, convenience stores, fitness centers, and doctors' offices.

Get Involved with Local Government

- Develop a local proclamation.
- Organize town meetings around your campaign message.
- Partner with community coalitions.
- Involve public housing projects.
- Involve the sheriff and youth probation services.
- Place posters in the Department of Motor Vehicles, police stations, or other high-visibility government locations.
- Develop banners for use in public spaces (e.g., on buildings and over roadways downtown).

Host Promotional Events

- Develop unique promotional products and distribute them at events which will draw your target audience.
- Organize giveaways that reward people for knowing the campaign message and facts.
- Create coffee mugs, posters, footballs, water bottles, hats, tee shirts, or other items bearing your campaign message. Carefully choose the events and places at which you distribute campaign-related merchandise to maximize audience exposure.

Your normative messages and pilot materials must be tested with your target population for believability and appeal. Focus groups and other strategies become a key resource for gathering input and information.

Pilot testing is part of the ongoing piloting and refining process that is essential to any social norms campaign. Pilot testing gives you a preview of how your messages will be received, and helps you ensure they will be understandable, credible and appealing to your target audience.

STEP 5.1 *TARGET TESTING*

Focus groups are extremely useful for testing specific campaign tools (such as posters, images, promotional items, and messages) and for gathering general information about your target audience (such as what sources they trust for health-related information and where they spend their time). Focus groups are one way you can "take the pulse" of the public conversation about driving after drinking, and determine how your materials can help steer it towards correcting misperceptions.

Start by testing your pilot ads with focus groups that represent the diversity of your target population. In these early groups, make sure to test **"The Three Ms"**:

1. Message. Test the content and wording of your normative message. Include:

- ✓ Understandability
- ✓ Clarity
- ✓ Appeal

2. Messenger. Test the way in which your message is presented. Include:

- ✓ Colors
- ✓ Logos
- ✓ Graphic design and images
- ✓ Types of models, actors and characters (e.g., male/female, old/young) they find most trustworthy and appealing

3. Medium. Test the ways you can get your message out. Include:

☑ Where they get their information (TV, radio, newspaper, word of mouth)

☑ What sources they find most trustworthy

In other words, ask your target audience 1) what they want to hear, 2) who they want to hear it from, and 3) how they want to hear it. Focus groups are where you will learn about the specific likes, dislikes and quirks of your target audience, and begin to understand their unique culture. This information and insight will help you design a campaign that is credible and appealing to them.

» *See Appendix F for sample focus group questions.*
» *See Appendix G for a sample focus group consent form.*

SOCIAL NORMS FOCUS GROUPS

During your focus groups, remember that you are testing your social norms messages, not social norms science. Compare it to this: when General Motors runs focus groups, it does not ask consumers to help them design a new exhaust system or engine. It asks them about their preferences in paint colors and cup holders, about the cosmetics and accessories that they find appealing. Likewise, you should not ask a focus group, "do you believe that a positive, normative campaign will correct your misperceptions and change your behavior?" Instead, you should use your focus group to collect information that will help you increase the appeal, credibility and noticeability of your campaign, and devise strategies to best jump-start the public dialogue.

Don't worry if the initial believability of your normative messages seems distressingly low. Remember that the people in your focus groups are going to be voicing the very misperceptions you are trying to change. Understand that your focus group participants are subject to the common myths and confusions that your goal it is to correct. Do not change your campaign to accommodate them, or lose faith in the positive, normative approach.

STEP 5.2 *STAKEHOLDER TESTING*

Test your preliminary messages with colleagues, key stakeholders and non-target community members to assess how they will react to the campaign. Focus groups or structured interviews with members of these groups can reveal any potentially controversial material you may have unintentionally included in your ad.

Stakeholder testing groups include:

- Law enforcement
- Local DUI taskforce
- ER doctors
- Funders
- Politicians
- Parents
- Youth
- Groups in close association with the target group

STEP 5.3 *SATURATION OF TESTING*

When your testing ceases to produce new, significant information and the results grow consistent, you have reached "saturation" and the pilot testing phase is complete. Now it is time to review and employ your results.

1. Examine the results of your pretesting and identify the most consistent criticisms and suggestions.

2. Refine your campaign message, tweak the look of your pilot ads, or amend your implementation strategy, as necessary.

3. Make note of any comments or concerns which you were not able to address. Keep these in mind for future ads and materials.

4. Develop a one page *executive summary* of your revised campaign message, materials and strategy. Return to members of your target population and key stakeholders with this executive summary and your revised campaign materials for a final check. Confirm that you have made changes that address their concerns.

STEP 5.4 *ONGOING DEVELOPMENT AND TESTING*

Resources allowing, you will repeat this process of testing and refining for every poster, newspaper ad, billboard or television advertisement that you create. Remember that you can test several ads during one focus group, and that you can test ads that are still in development. You may want to test a television ad that is still in script form or at the rough cut stage. You can even create a "dummy" ad using film clips taken from the web that will give your testers an idea of the look, feel or story of a commercial you have not yet made.

MOST of Us Tip: Be "PC"

Use your testing to make sure that your ads avoid racial and gender stereotypes, as well as other politically divisive behaviors such as littering or biking without a helmet. It is important that all of your materials be "politically correct" on every level.

ANATOMY OF A SOCIAL NORMS TELEVISION COMMERCIAL

Like all of your social norms materials (and unlike most of what you see on TV) the television commercials that you develop should be positive, inclusive and empowering.

Your TV ads should include:

✓ **Your normative message**

✓ **Statistics or numbers from your survey**

✓ **A credible data source**

✓ **A recognizable logo**

✓ **An engaging photo**

✓ **Funder's logo**

✓ **Your website address**

✓ **Necessary disclaimers (such as "Any amount of alcohol may be illegal or dangerous" if you are targeting drivers below the legal drinking age)**

Visit **mostofus.org** to view television commercials created by MOST of Us.

IMPLEMENT THE CAMPAIGN

Campaign implementation is the job of running and troubleshooting your campaign on a daily basis. It includes placing print and broadcast media messages, running local activities that promote your social norms messages, and managing your campaign's interaction with your target audience and the community at large.

STEP 6.1 *PLACE MEDIA*

Your media firm should place your television and radio ads, and send you weekly updates to show that they ran on schedule. It is your job to place all of your other advertising in accordance with your market plan. Some suggestions and guidelines:

Placing Newspaper Ads

- Ask for non-profit rates.

- Place your ads on the paper's high circulations days. The increase in readership is usually worth the added cost.

- Consider your audience. Should your ad be in the sports section or the entertainment section?

- Request that your ad not be placed near ads for alcohol or bars.

- Placing ads in high school and college papers is inexpensive and a great way to get your message out to younger audiences.

Placing Billboard Ads

- Ask for non-profit rates.

- Request data on estimated daily circulation.

- Some vendors offer "space available" contracts. These are great for large campaign areas with broad target groups. You pay for a vinyl billboard to be printed, then the vendor places it in their service area on empty billboards waiting to be sold. Your billboard will move around the area, allowing a greater number of individuals to see your message.

Placing Movie Theater Slides

- Ask for non-profit rates.

- There is usually only one company that places theater slides (the advertising stills shown onscreen before a movie starts) in each theater complex. Call your local movie theaters for the name and number of those companies.

- Ask for information regarding the number of times your slide(s) will show before each movie. Information about the length of time people sit before a movie starts may also be available.

STEP 6.2 PREPARE FOR PUBLIC RESPONSE

Once your media campaign launches, your dialogue with your target audience and the community at large begins. Holding up your end of this public conversation is part of your continuing campaign management. Responding to critics, educating potential supporters, and cultivating community understanding and acceptance will be ongoing and critical projects.

No matter how much careful planning and focus group testing you have done, no matter how well you think you understand your target audience and the types of reactions your message will elicit, everything changes when your campaign "goes live." It is impossible to predict the reaction your campaign will elicit. The only thing to be sure of is that the community will react, and you must be prepared with strong communication skills and strategies.

At first, some people will not believe or like your message. Prepare for that, and embrace it as part of the process. People are very attached to their misperceptions, and will distrust any information that proves them false. A social norms campaign is a confrontational process, as your positive messages collide with the widespread misperceptions of the public at large.

MOST of Us Tip: Slow and Steady Wins the Race

While nothing beats the drama of a big, splashy launch, it is wise to roll out your campaign slowly. Build interest and "tease" your campaign over time—this will allow you to get feedback from the public before you have committed all of your resources. You don't want to put all of your energy and resources into a single message only to find that it has missed the mark.

MOST of Us Tip: Avoid Project Paralysis

We have seen campaign planners freeze right before their campaign is supposed to go live. Dreading potential negative feedback, they stall and delay. Negative feedback is part of the process, and your campaign will never be perfect. Stay on schedule and have the courage to take your campaign live.

STEP 6.3 *PILOTING ON THE RUN*

Rest assured that once you go live, things will not go as planned. Television stations will run the wrong ads, vendors' prices will be thousands of dollars higher than promised, delays will wreak havoc with your schedule. Get ready to take on a new role as damage controller and troubleshooter, and be willing to let go of some of your ideas about how your campaign is going to run. You will have to be prepared to react quickly, change plans on the fly, and effectively pilot your project on the run.

The good news is that unexpected ways to strengthen and bolster your campaign will arise as well. Before your launch, most people will not know you exist; afterwards, individuals and groups with compatible interests and goals will contact you with unforeseen opportunities for increasing exposure and building partnerships. Remain flexible and open to new these new possibilities; partnerships can be a very valuable way to expand the reach, increase the sustainability, or share the "ownership" of your campaign.

STEP 6.4 *COLLECTING DATA FOR NEXT GENERATION MESSAGES*

Pay attention to the response your campaign receives from your target audience and the community at large. These reactions—both positive and negative—are valuable data that will help you craft your "next generation" of messages.

Listen to and watch your audience closely, archiving the data you collect. Keep defaced campaign posters, letters to the editor of the local papers, transcripts of phone calls your campaign office receives. Look for patterns and themes. If you can anticipate the direction of the public conversation about your campaign, you can design messages that will help you steer that conversation where you would like it to go.

STEP 6.5 *A POSITIVE SPIN ON NEGATIVE PRESS*

They say there is no such thing as bad publicity; we say there is no such thing as negative press. In fact, if you are not hearing negative feedback, you have cause for worry, since it likely means your messages are not being disseminated at a sufficient dosage. Negative feedback indicates that you are on your way to meeting your first goal, which is achieving a critical mass of campaign awareness.

Learn to think positively about negative press. Every time your campaign is blasted in the media, you are given another opportunity to educate the community about social norms and to reframe the public conversation about driving after drinking. Take advantage of these opportunities. Write op-eds and letters to the editor, schedule television and radio talk show appearances. Use these opportunities to clarify and promote your message.

Train your eye to look for media coverage which reinforces misperceptions about driving after drinking. An article headlined, "Driving after Drinking at Epidemic Levels" provides the opportunity to educate people about misperceptions and actual norms.

Confusing messages lead to negative press.

Some thoughts on dealing with negative press:

• You must respond to it. If you don't frame your campaign and clarify its purpose and meaning, someone else will.

• It is sometimes stronger to have someone else—a law enforcement official, key stakeholder or partnering group—respond on your behalf. This will help you avoid sounding defensive, and show that your campaign has support from key community members or groups.

• Restate your campaign's core value, such as: "We all agree that we must reduce driving after drinking."

• Just like your messages, your responses to criticism should always be positive. Don't sink to finger-pointing or name-calling. Acknowledge the criticism and simply clarify any misperceptions of your message (e.g. "Great point, here's a clarification of the social norms process…" or "Social norms is not what we're accustomed to, but this is why this kind of effort has worked in the past, and why we need it here.")

Some specific points you might want to make include:

• Positive social norms messages do not sugar-coat driving after drinking, or minimize its seriousness. Social norms theory holds that we can acknowledge problems while promoting the existing healthy behaviors that inhibit them. By focusing on positive norms, social norms campaigns can create even more protective standards of behavior.

• Driving after drinking is a problem that is 100% preventable.

For more on dealing with the press, download The Main Frame at **mostofus.org**.

STEP 6.6 *DEVELOP A COMMUNICATIONS PLAN*

A well-designed communications plan can ensure that your organization has a strong public image and that your campaign and its goals are well understood. It will also give you the tools to interact with the public and to respond to both the support and the criticism your campaign will receive.

A strong communications plan can help you:

- ✓ Increase your campaign's visibility and promote recognition of your message
- ✓ Generate positive media coverage of your campaign and its activities
- ✓ Reach influential individuals and organizations
- ✓ Influence public opinion
- ✓ Increase awareness of driving after drinking issues
- ✓ Create support for legislative change
- ✓ Generate support from funders, policymakers and community members
- ✓ Leverage existing resources by partnering with other government agencies, community groups, law enforcement and local businesses

Specific elements of your communications plan should include:

- ✓ Developing relationships with key stakeholders
- ✓ Developing relationships with reporters and editors
- ✓ Implementing strategies for marketing your campaign message
- ✓ Creating a calendar of campaign events
- ✓ Planning news-generating events at key points during campaign
- ✓ Distributing news releases before significant campaign developments
- ✓ Pitching feature stories about charismatic elements of your campaign
- ✓ Writing opinion pieces and op-eds
- ✓ Writing timely and concise letters to the editor
- ✓ Scheduling regular appearances on television and radio talk shows

COMMUNICATION ESSENTIALS

There are four basic materials you will need before you start your communications outreach. These will form the basis of the press kits you send to the media, community partners, and other key stakeholders in your campaign, and will help you tell a reporter or other interested party exactly how you want your group, campaign, and effort to be described. They are:

1. A general press release about your campaign that you can adapt for various events and announcements.

2. A brochure about your organization and campaign.

3. A sheet of facts and message points that briefly and accurately outline the essentials of your campaign. These should be quotable "sound bites" that you can deliver to the media or use to explain your campaign to others in the community. This fact sheet should cover the method and essential message of your campaign, background on driving after drinking in your state, as well as the basics of social norms theory.

4. A one-page "crisis response sheet" to use if a driving after drinking tragedy occurs during your campaign. Disproportionate media attention to high-profile tragedy crisis can further reinforce misperceptions and heighten scrutiny of your campaign. Being prepared beforehand will allow you to respond quickly and calmly.

For each item in your plan, outline who is responsible for the task, when it needs to be carried out, and what its budget limitations are.

» *See Appendix H for tips on developing media and community relationships.*
» *See Appendix I for tips on writing and submitting an op-ed.*
» *See Appendix J for a sample op-ed.*
» *See Appendix K for tips on writing and submitting a press release.*

The social norms marketing process is driven by continual evaluation of campaign effectiveness. Quantitative and qualitative data are gathered, analyzed, and fed back into the campaign to refine its implementation.

Countless books, experts, and conferences have been dedicated to evaluation—all of which can leave you overwhelmed, if not in complete project paralysis.

The beauty of a well-implemented social norms program is that evaluation occurs *throughout* the implementation process. If you follow Steps 1 through 6 of this Toolkit, you almost don't need Step 7; your evaluation is simply a continuation of the data-driven work you have been doing from the start. As you run your focus groups, gather survey data, and collect quantitative and qualitative data on the reaction to your campaign, you will use this information to improve your campaign's messages and methodologies. Document this process as you go, and you will find your project evaluation and write-up much, much easier.

STEP 7.1 FORMATIVE EVALUATION

There are four major types of evaluation: formative evaluation, process evaluation, outcome evaluation and impact evaluation.

Formative evaluation is all of the research and information-gathering you do during the development and planning of your project. This may include literature reviews, meetings with key stakeholders, and technical assistance you receive from MOST of Us or others who have implemented similar programs. Formative evaluation helps you to determine 1) which elements are required for your project to be successful and 2) if all of those elements are in place before you begin.

You can think of your formative evaluation as a review and assessment of all of the work you did in Steps 1 and 2. Did you…

? Set the right goals for your project?

? Select the correct target audience?

? Choose correct intervention and control areas?

? Schedule an appropriate timeline?

? Secure sufficient funding?

? Hire the right administrative and management team?

? Design an appropriate survey and survey administration plan?

? Properly analyze your baseline data?

STEP 7.2 *PROCESS EVALUATION*

Process evaluation happens as you are implementing your project. It determines whether your campaign is being implemented with the quality, intensity, and fidelity necessary to get results. Are campaign materials being distributed to the right people, at the right intensity? Are program activities occurring as planned?

Process evaluation assesses the work you did in Steps 3, 4 and 5. Did you...

? Develop appropriate messages for your target audience?

? Develop a market plan that successfully delivered these messages?

THE DAYTIMER EXERCISE

Check your DayTimer (or calendar or Palm Pilot or wall of Post-It notes): Are you living in a black hole? Look at the past month of appointments and meetings and add up how much time you spent on each aspect of your campaign. It's important to make sure you are working to move all of your objectives forward, and not getting stuck.

Don't reinvent the wheel. Are you spending months developing a new survey when a phone call could get an existing one? Pay attention to what's worked for other people who've tried similar things. Listen to those who've been there before you.

Are you and your staff always in meetings, or chained to the copy machine? The administrative, behind-the-scenes tasks you do are important, but they do not work towards changing the perceptions and behaviors of your target audience. The DayTimer exercise is a way to make sure most of your time and resources are going towards your goal.

What really matters at the end of the day is translating data into messages and getting the messages out with enough exposure to create results. That's the heart of the process, and you have to keep it beating.

? Conduct appropriate pilot testing?

? Use the results to improve your messages and market plan?

STEP 7.3 OUTCOME EVALUATION

Outcome evaluation is based on the results of your follow-up surveys, and assesses whether your campaign achieved its stated goals and objectives. For example, if your goal was to reduce the self-reported frequency of driving after drinking in western Montana by 5% after a one-year social norms marketing campaign, your follow-up surveys should clearly show whether or not you were successful, or how close you came to your goal.

Outcome evaluation corresponds with Step 6, and generally means evaluating whether you ran your media at the frequency and intensity required to 1) change perceptions and 2) change behavior and attitudes. It involves three key evaluation questions, as outlined in the chart below:

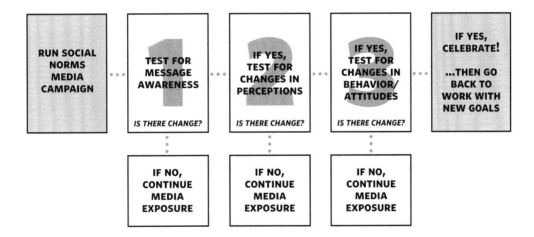

The second and third questions are dependent upon the first: if adequate message exposure is not achieved, perceptions will not change, and if perceptions do not change, neither will attitudes or behavior. Conversely, if you find behavioral change without message awareness or changes in perception, you cannot claim your intervention played a role in that change. This is why outcome evaluation is key. Did you…

? Make your target group aware of the campaign messages?

? Change their perceptions?

? Change their behavior?

? Change their attitudes?

? Impact the public conversation?

STEP 7.4 *IMPACT EVALUATION*

Impact evaluation uses external measures to assess whether your program had an impact on rates of driving after drinking.

At the outset of your study, you looked to outside sources of data to get the most accurate picture of your target audience and their involvement in driving after drinking (see Step 2.8). To conduct your impact evaluation, you should return to these same sources of data. Did the number or rate of fatal driving after drinking crashes drop during or after your campaign? The frequency of alcohol-related crashes? The number of DUI arrests? See if these or other markers of driving after drinking in your target group can support or substantiate the measured results of your campaign.

You should also examine your documents notebook (see Step 1.9) to see if media coverage of driving after drinking changed during the course of your campaign to reflect a more positive framing of the issue.

In addition, the qualitative information in your documents notebook should confirm that other related environmental conditions held constant during the course of your campaign, and that no new prevention campaign, enforcement measure, or high-profile accident could be responsible for measured changes in your target audience.

GOODBYE AND GOOD LUCK

If you've gotten this far, you are as ready to get started as you'll ever be. So do it. Start. Push forward, stay positive, get results—and share them with others in the field. For support and advice from others who are implementing social norms programs, join the MOST of Us online community at **communities.mostofus.org**.

REFERENCES

Berkowitz, A. D. (2004). Emerging challenges and issues for the social norms approach. *The Report on Social Norms*, 3(7), 1.

Berkowitz, A. D. (2004). *The social norms approach: theory, research and annotated bibliography*. Retrieved August 8, 2004, from the website for the Higher Education Center: www.edc.org/hec/socialnorms/

Cialdini, R. B. (2003). Crafting normative messages to protect the environment. *Current Directions in Psychological Science*, 12(4), 105-109.

Haines, M.P. (1996). *A social norms approach to preventing binge drinking at colleges and universities*. Newton, MA: Higher Education Center for Alcohol and Drug Prevention.

Linkenbach, J.W. (1999, September). *Social norms marketing: The science of promoting healthy norms to improve health outcomes through community campaigns*. Presented at the State Conference on Social Norms Marketing, Helena, MT.

Linkenbach, J. W. (2001). Cultural cataracts: Identifying and correcting misperceptions in the media. *The Report on Social Norms*. Working Paper #1.

Linkenbach, J. W. (2003). The Montana model: Development and overview of a seven-step process for implementing macro-level social norms campaigns. In H. W. Perkins (Ed.), *The social norms approach to preventing school and college age substance abuse* (pp.182-205). San Francisco, CA: Jossey-Bass.

Linkenbach, J. W. (2003, May). MOST of Us®: *The science of the positive*. Keynote presentation to the National Canadian BACCHUS Conference, Toronto, ONT, Canada.

Linkenbach, J.W., and Perkins, H.W. (2003a). Misperceptions of peer alcohol norms in a statewide survey of young adults. In H. W. Perkins (Ed.), *The social norms approach to preventing school and college age substance abuse* (pp. 173-181). San Francisco, CA: Jossey-Bass.

Linkenbach, J., and Perkins, H.W. (2003b). MOST of Us® are tobacco free: An eight-month social norms campaign reducing youth initiation of smoking in Montana. In H.W. Perkins (Ed.), *The social norms approach to preventing school and college age substance abuse* (pp. 224-234). San Francisco, CA: Jossey-Bass.

Linkenbach, J. W. and Perkins, H.W. (in press). *MOST of Us prevent drinking and driving: A successful social norms campaign to reduce driving after drinking among young adults in western Montana* (DOT publication HS 809 869). Washington, DC: National Highway Traffic Safety Administration.

Continued on following page

Malenfant, L., Wells, J., Van Houten, R., and Williams, A. (1996). The use of feedback signs to increase observed daytime seat belt use in two cities in North Carolina. *Accident Analysis and Prevention*, 28(6), 771-777.

National Highway Traffic Safety Administration. (2000). *National survey of drinking and driving attitudes and behavior: 1999, Volume 1: Findings* (DOT HS 809 190). Washington, DC: National Highway Traffic Safety Administration.

Perkins, H.W. (1997). College student misperceptions of alcohol and other drug norms among peers: Exploring causes, consequences, and implications for prevention programs. In *Designing alcohol and other drug prevention programs in higher education* (pp. 177-206). Newton, MA: The Higher Education Center for Alcohol and Other Drug Prevention.

Perkins, H.W., and Berkowitz, A. D. (1986). Perceiving the community norms of alcohol use among students: Some research implications for campus alcohol education programming. *International Journal of the Addictions*, 21, 961-976.

Perkins, H.W. (2003). The emergence and evolution of the social norms approach to substance abuse prevention. In H.W. Perkins (Ed.) *The social norms approach to preventing school and college age substance abuse* (pp. 3-17). San Francisco, CA: Jossey-Bass.

Perkins, H.W., and Craig, D. (2003). The imaginary lives of peers: Patterns of substance use and misperceptions of norms among secondary school students. In H.W. Perkins (Ed.), *The social norms approach to preventing school and college age substance abuse* (pp. 209-223). San Francisco, CA: Jossey-Bass.

APPENDIX A

SIX-MONTH CAMPAIGN SNAPSHOT

MARCH	APRIL	MAY
week 1 **Mar. 1: CAMPAIGN BEGINS** **Mar. 1: TRAINING** social norms training.	**week 1** **Apr. 1-May 30: TV AND RADIO ADS** Television and radio stations will donate free airtime to broadcast statewide public service announcements. **Apr. 1-May 30: TV AND RADIO ADS** cont. **Mar. 8-Apr. 20: MEDIA ADVOCACY** cont.	**week 1** **May 1: MAY MOBILIZATION** Retrofit the press releases NHTSA has created with the social norms messages and send them out. **Apr. 30-May 9: POSTERS** cont. **Apr. 1-May 30: TV AND RADIO ADS** cont.
week 2 **Mar. 8-Apr. 20: MEDIA ADVOCACY** Focus on media advocacy efforts by writing a newspaper op-ed or letters to the editor. Pitch local newspapers, radio and television stations on stories that highlight the activities or reflect the philosophy of the overall campaign.	**week 2** **Apr. 1-May 30: TV AND RADIO ADS** cont. **Mar. 8-Apr. 20: MEDIA ADVOCACY** cont.	**week 2** **May 10-17: GYM TOWELS** Place towels with campaign messages printed on them in local gyms (YMCA, school gyms, health clubs, community swimming pools, etc.). **Apr. 1-May 30: TV AND RADIO ADS** cont. **Apr. 30-May 9: POSTERS** ends.
week 3 **Mar. 8-Apr. 20: MEDIA ADVOCACY** cont. **Mar.8-Apr. 20: SECURE PARTNERSHIPS** with local business owners to participate in featured efforts (i.e. spring break, St. Patrick's day, May Mobilization, etc.). **Mar. 17: ST. PATRICK'S DAY** March with posters or attend a community event. Have a local business donate Irish-themed prizes and give them away to people who can recite your campaign statistic.	**week 3** **Apr. 1-May 30: TV AND RADIO ADS** cont. **Mar. 8-Apr. 20: MEDIA ADVOCACY** ends.	**week 3** **May 10-17: GYM TOWELS** ends. **Apr. 1-May 30: TV AND RADIO ADS** cont.
week 4 **Mar. 8-Apr. 20: MEDIA ADVOCACY** cont.	**week 4** **Apr. 23-30: SCHOOL ACTIVITIES** Schools will be breaking for summer vacation so it's important to get into schools (if the students are part of your target audience). Set up an informational assembly to tell students about the campaign. Give out promotional items to students who quote the campaign message accurately. Put posters on campus. **Apr. 1-May 30: TV AND RADIO ADS** cont.	**week 4** **May 21-28: NAPKINS** Give napkins printed with the campaign message to places around your community that are frequented by your target audience (fast food restaurants, ice cream stores, delis, bars, school cafeterias, community picnics and street fairs, etc.). **Apr. 1-May 30: TV AND RADIO ADS** cont.
week 5 **Mar. 8-Apr. 20: MEDIA ADVOCACY** cont.	**week 5** **Apr. 30-May 9: POSTERS** Distribute posters and hang them in high visibility public areas (banks, convenience stores, public library, the DMV, gas stations, Laundromats, college campuses, restaurants, pubs, etc.) **Apr. 1-May 30: TV AND RADIO ADS** cont. **Apr. 23-30: SCHOOL ACTIVITIES** ends.	**week 5** **May 21-28: NAPKINS** ends. **May 29-June 5: MAIN STREET DISPLAY** Create an elaborate display that features your campaign posters and promotional items in the window of a main street business (bank, variety store, vacant building, etc.). **Apr. 1-May 30: TV AND RADIO ADS** ends.

Continued on following page

SIX-MONTH CAMPAIGN SNAPSHOT (CONTINUED)

JUNE	JULY	AUGUST
weeks 1 and 2 **June 6-13: SUMMER FAIR PRIZE GIVEAWAY** Take advantage of a summer fair or festival to spread the message. Get the fair sponsors to advertise that people will have the opportunity to win prizes at the fair if they can quote the statistic used in the campaign. **Sidewalk Chalk Talk** is a fun opportunity for youth to write messages relating to the campaign on the sidewalks in the vicinity of the fair or festival grounds. **Post flyers** announcing the prizes to be given at the fair. Buy **gift certificates** (for pizza or CDs) and offer them as prizes along with campaign promotional items. Send one of your representatives roaming around the fair to ask people to cite the statistic featured in the campaign and award them with a gift certificate if they can do so. Set up an **information booth** that prominently displays your posters and various promotional items. Answer questions that the public may have and give them additional information about the campaign.	**week 1** **July 1-Aug. 30: RADIO AD** Another radio PSA will be running on local stations. **July 2-8: 4th OF JULY** Set up a booth and decorate it with campaign posters. Distribute free lemonade and ice water in cups with the campaign message on it at fireworks displays, at parks, and at picnics. **June 25-July2: LOCAL BUSINESS MARQUEE DISPLAYS** ends.	**week 1** **July 1-Aug. 30: RADIO AD** cont. **July 26-Aug. 2: POSTER AND PENCIL GIVEAWAY** ends.
	week 2 **July 10-17: POSTERS** Distribute posters and put them in high visibility public areas that were not covered in the first round of distribution (town hall, police stations, doctors' offices, malls, grocery stores, etc.) Make sure posters put up earlier in campaign are still up. **July 1-Aug. 30: RADIO AD** cont.	**week 2** **Aug. 6-Aug. 13: MAIN STREET DISPLAY** Create another elaborate display that features your campaign posters and promotional items in the window of a main street business (bank, variety store, vacant building, etc.) **July 1-Aug. 30: RADIO AD** cont.
week 3 **June 14-21: PENCIL GIVEAWAY** During a high-traffic community event (a big sale at the mall, a sidewalk sale downtown, a rodeo, a picnic) either set up a booth or roam around and give out pencils to the public while talking about the campaign. **June 6-13: SUMMER FAIR PRIZE GIVEAWAY** ends.	**week 3** **July 18-25: CUP DISTRIBUTION** Give cups with the campaign slogan on them to various restaurants and bars around the community (fast food restaurants, pubs, ice cream stores, etc.). **July 1-Aug. 30: RADIO AD** cont. **July 10-17: POSTERS** ends.	**week 3** **Aug. 14-21: TABLE TENTS** Distribute table tents and place them on tables in high visibility areas (school cafeterias, public library, restaurants, bars, convenience stories, laundromats, etc.) **July 1-Aug. 30: RADIO AD** cont. **Aug. 6-Aug. 13: MAIN STREET DISPLAY** ends.
week 4 **June 14-21: PENCIL GIVEAWAY** ends.	**week 4** **July 26-Aug. 2: POSTER AND PENCIL GIVEAWAY** Place posters in stores and restaurants around the community and ask them to giveaway pencils with your campaign slogan on them to customers at the cash register. **July 1-Aug. 30: RADIO AD** cont. **July 18-25: CUP DISTRIBUTION** ends.	**week 4** **Aug. 22-29: SCHOOL ACTIVITIES** Schools (particularly colleges) will be going back into session soon. Plan events for college orientation week (ads in school newspaper, flyers, promo item giveaway, booth at orientation fair, posters up on campus, etc.) **July 1-Aug. 30: RADIO AD** cont. **Aug. 14-21: TABLE TENTS** ends.
week 5 **June 25-July 2: LOCAL BUSINESS MARQUEE DISPLAYS** Ask local businesses to donate their marquee signs and write your campaign message on them (movie theaters, garages, car washes, schools, fair grounds, hotels, restaurants, etc.).	**week 5** **July 1-Aug. 30: RADIO AD** cont. **July 26-Aug. 2: POSTER AND PENCIL GIVEAWAY** cont.	**week 5** **Aug. 30-Sept. 6: LABOR DAY ACTIVITIES** Donate cups and napkins that have the campaign message on them to community fairs or picnics that are taking place over the holiday weekend. **July 1-Aug. 30: RADIO AD** ends.

APPENDIX B

CAMPAIGN BUDGET OUTLINE AND WORKSHEET

BUDGET OUTLINE

Use the chart below to outline a budget that meets all of our staffing, administrative, and project needs. Add and amend categories as necessary.

LINE ITEM	BUDGET	STAFF PERSON, COMPANY, or ACTIVITY DESCRIPTION
SALARIES/BENEFITS		
Project Manager		
Project Manager Benefits		
Project Coordinator		
Project Coordinator Benefits		
Administrator		
Administrator Benefits		
TOTAL SALARY		
TOTAL BENEFITS		
TOTAL SALARY AND BENEFITS		
CONTRACTED/SUBCONTRACTED SERVICES		
Survey Development		*Purchase or development of campaign survey*
Survey Administration		*Web, phone, mail or other administration process*
Data Analysis		
Media Development		*Production of radio and TV advertisements*
Media Purchase		*Placement of paid TV and radio ads*
Graphic Design		*Organization logo, newspaper ads, campaign posters*
Marketing Consultants		
Media Duplication Costs		*Duplication of radio and TV ads*
CD Duplication		
Print Duplication		*Duplication of posters, reports to funders*
TOTAL CONTRACTED SERVICES		
SUPPLIES/EXPENDABLES		
Office Supplies		*Paper, pens, notebooks*
Promotional Items		*Imprinted items for giveaways and contests*
Newspaper Advertisements		*Fees for ad space*
TOTAL SUPPLIES		
EQUIPMENT		
Equipment Purchase		*Computers, computer hardware, copier, fax*
Equipment Maintenance		
Software		
TOTAL EQUIPMENT		

Continued on following page

BUDGET OUTLINE (CONTINUED)

LINE ITEM	BUDGET	STAFF PERSON, COMPANY, OR ACTIVITY DESCRIPTION
COMMUNICATIONS		
Postage/Delivery		
Telephone/Fax/Email		
TOTAL COMMUNICATIONS		
TRAVEL		
Travel Costs		*Airfare, hotels, meals*
TOTAL TRAVEL		
TOTAL COSTS		

BUDGET WORKSHEET: STAFF TIME

Use the chart below to approximate the amount of staff time that will be required to complete your project. Estimate the amount of time that each staff member will spend on each project task—try to be exhaustive in generating task categories. Calculate time in hours per week or weeks per year, whichever makes the estimation easier.

WORK CATEGORY	STAFF MEMBERS (LIST NAMES IN ROW BELOW)				
Survey Development					
Human Subjects					
Enter Survey Online					
Internal Testing					
Survey Report					
Message Development					
Media Development					
Media Production					
Media Placement					
Focus Group (set up, conduct, report)					
Print Materials Development					
Promo Development					
Newspaper Ad Placement					
Technology Development					
Technology Production					
Site Visits					
Phone Consultation					
Report Writing					
Report Editing					
Media Advocacy					

Hello, my name is _____ and I am calling because you have been selected to participate in a survey sponsored by _____. _____ is conducting a study of alcohol consumption among Montana's young adult population. Your telephone number was randomly selected by a computer and all answers to this survey will remain anonymous.

In order to interview the right person, I need to speak to a member of your household who is between the ages of 21 and 34. Would that be you?

Before we begin, I want you to know that your honest responses are very important to the project. If you do not know or are not sure how to answer a question, just respond "I don't know." You will be asked questions about your personal behavior regarding alcohol consumption. The survey takes about 12 minutes, and your comments will be kept confidential and anonymous. Your participation in this survey is completely voluntary and you may end this interview at any time.

Question Age
First, how old are you? _____

▶ IF THERE IS NO ONE IN THE HOUSEHOLD WHO IS BETWEEN 21 AND 34, RECORD AS CODE "NO ONE 21-34". IF THE 21-34 YEAR OLD IS NOT HOME, CODE FOR CALLBACK.

Question OK
Do you agree to participate in this survey?   1. Yes   2. No

▶ IF ANSWER IS YES, GO TO **Question Sex**. IF ANSWER IS NO, END THE CALL BY SAYING "Thank you for your time," AND HANGING UP.

Question Sex
Respondents sex? (ASK if not obvious)   1. Male   2. Female

SECTION I: SOCIAL NORMS

We want to begin by asking some questions about your perceptions of other Montanans and their alcohol consumption. We just want your impressions of what others do. For the purpose of this survey, A DRINK IS considered to be ONE 12-OUNCE BEER, ONE GLASS OF WINE, ONE MIXED DRINK OR ONE SHOT of liquor.

Question AvMtDays
On how many days in a typical month do you think the average Montanan your age consumes alcoholic beverages? _____

Question AvMlDays
How about the average Male? _____

Question AvFmDays

How about the average Female? _____

▶ TYPE IN THEIR ANSWER AND PRESS ENTER. USE 99 FOR DON'T KNOW OR NO RESPONSE (DK-NR).
IF THEY SAY THEY DON'T KNOW, ENCOURAGE THEM TO TAKE A GUESS.

Question AvFem2Wk

In the past two weeks how often do you think the average Montana female your age has had 4 or more
drinks at one time? _____

▶ TYPE IN THEIR ANSWER AND PRESS ENTER. USE 99 FOR DK-NR.
IF THEY SAY THEY DON'T KNOW, ENCOURAGE THEM TO TAKE A GUESS.

Question AvMal2Wk

In the past two weeks how often do you think the average Montana male your age has had 5 or more
drinks at one time? _____

▶ TYPE IN THEIR ANSWER AND PRESS ENTER. USE 99 FOR DK-NR.
IF THEY SAY THEY DON'T KNOW, ENCOURAGE THEM TO TAKE A GUESS.

Question AvMtDriv

During the past month, do you think the average Montanan your age has driven within one hour after consuming
2 or more alcoholic beverages within an hour?

        1. Yes   2. No   99. DK-NR

▶ IF THEY SAY THEY DON'T KNOW, ENCOURAGE THEM TO TAKE A GUESS.

Question AvFemDr

In the past month, what percentage of Montana female drivers your age do you think drove within one hour after
they consumed 2 or more drinks within one hour? _____

Question AvMaleDr

How about male drivers your age? _____

▶ TYPE IN THEIR ANSWER AND PRESS ENTER. USE 99 FOR DK-NR.
IF THEY SAY THEY DON'T KNOW, ENCOURAGE THEM TO TAKE A GUESS.

Question AvMtDD

In your opinion, among Montanans your age who drink, what percentage almost always make sure they
have a designated, non-drinking driver with them before they consume any alcohol and will be riding in
a car later? _____

▶ TYPE IN THEIR ANSWER AND PRESS ENTER. USE 99 FOR DK-NR.
IF THEY SAY THEY DON'T KNOW, ENCOURAGE THEM TO TAKE A GUESS.

Question BAC

The current law in Montana states that a blood alcohol concentration above .10% (point one zero percent) constitutes legal impairment. Would you support or oppose changing the law in Montana to make a blood alcohol concentration above .08% (point zero eight percent) constitute legal impairment? This change would permit less alcohol consumption before driving.

1. Support   2. Oppose   99. DK-NR

Question AvMTBAC

About what percentage of 21 to 34 year old Montanans do you think would favor changing the legal limit for blood alcohol concentration from .10% (point one zero percent) down to .08% (point zero eight percent)? _____

▶ TYPE IN THEIR ANSWER AND PRESS ENTER. USE 99 FOR DK-NR.
IF THEY SAY THEY DON'T KNOW, ENCOURAGE THEM TO TAKE A GUESS.

Question OpenCont

Montana does not make it an offense to have an open alcoholic beverage container in a vehicle. Would you support or oppose a law to prohibit an open alcoholic beverage container and consumption of an alcoholic beverage in a vehicle on the public roadway?

1. Support   2. Oppose   99. DK-NR

Question AvMTOpenCont

Of 21- to 34-year-old Montanans, what percentage do you think would favor a law to prohibit an open alcoholic beverage container and consumption of an alcoholic beverage in a vehicle on the public roadway? _____

▶ TYPE IN THEIR ANSWER AND PRESS ENTER. USE 99 FOR DK-NR.
IF THEY SAY THEY DON'T KNOW, ENCOURAGE THEM TO TAKE A GUESS.

Question ProtDryes

In the past year, have you found yourself in the position of considering whether to ride in a car with a driver who had been drinking alcohol?

1. Yes (go to next question)   2. No (Skip to **Question OthInter**)

▶ IF YES...

Question ProtDrDr

The last time you found yourself in the position of considering whether to ride in a car with a driver who had been drinking alcohol, what did you do?

1. Walked
2. Went ahead and rode with the drinking driver
3. Used a taxi or other public transportation
4. Used a non-drinking designated driver
5. Called someone to pick you up
6. Asked around at the party or bar for a non-drinking driver
7. Selected the person you think has had the least to drink

Continued on following page

8. Other
99. DK-NR

Question OthInter

What percentage of Montanans your age do you think intervened the last time they encountered a situation where someone they knew had consumed 2 or more drinks within one hour and was going to drive? _____

▶ TYPE IN THEIR ANSWER AND PRESS ENTER. USE 99 FOR DK-NR.
IF THEY SAY THEY DON'T KNOW, ENCOURAGE THEM TO TAKE A GUESS.

SECTION II: MESSAGE EXPOSURE

Question AlPreAd

During the last twelve months, do you remember seeing or hearing any alcohol prevention campaign advertisements, posters, radio or TV commercials, or brochures?

1. Yes (Go to next question)
2. No (Skip to **Question AskMost**)
99. DK-NR

▶ IF YES...
During the last twelve months, how many times have you seen or heard these advertisements on...

Question TV ... television? _____
Question Radio ... radio? _____
Question ColNews ... college newspaper? _____
Question CityNews ... local non college newspaper? _____
Question Poster ... posters brochure, sign, etc.? _____
Question PrevOth ... other? _____

▶ TYPE IN THEIR ANSWER IF THEY HAVE ONE. IF THEY CAN ONLY GIVE A RANGE, THEN TYPE THE MIDPOINT OF THE RANGE.

Question Alrecent

When was the last time you saw or heard one of these advertisements?

1. Within the last 12 months, but not within the last month
2. Within the last month, but not within the last week
3. Within the last week
99. DK-NR

Question MainMess

What was the main message that you remember? DO NOT READ ANSWERS

1. Mentioned that most of us (or the majority of us, 4 out of 5, or 80% of us) drink moderately or not at all, that is four or less drinks at a time or once per week or less.
2. Mentioned that most of us (or the majority of us, 4 out of 5, or 80% of us) don't drink and drive.

3. Mentioned that most of us (or the majority of us, 4 out of 5, or 80% of us) drink four or less drinks at a time and also mentioned that most of us (or the majority of us, 4 out of 5, or 80% of us) don't drink and drive

4. Mentioned most of us (or majority) and using a designated driver.

5. Mentioned using a designated driver but did NOT mention most of us (or majority).

6. Other prevention message which does NOT include most of us (or the majority of us or 80% of us)

99. DK-NR

▶ IF RESPONSE TO **MainMess** <u>DOES</u> MENTION MOST OF US, OR THE MAJORITY OF US, 4 OUT OF 5, OR 80% OF US (RESPONSES 1, 2, 3, 4), GO TO **SECTION III** or **SECTION I INTRODUCTION**. IF RESPONSE TO **MainMess** DOES <u>NOT</u> MENTION MOST OF US, OR THE MAJORITY OF US, 4 OUT OF 5, OR 80% OF US (RESPONSES 5, 6, or 99), ASK **Question AskMost**.

Question AskMost
During the last 12 months do you remember seeing or hearing any alcohol prevention campaign advertisements mentioning most of us, the majority of us, 4 out of 5, or 80% of us, don't drink and drive, or use a designated driver?

1. Yes   2. No

SECTION III: ALCOHOL USE

The remainder of the survey is about your experiences with alcohol. Again, all your comments will be kept confidential and anonymous. And just as a reminder, A DRINK IS considered ONE 12-OUNCE BEER, ONE GLASS OF WINE, ONE MIXED DRINK OR ONE SHOT.

Question Meanmnth
About how many times have you consumed alcohol in the past month? _____

Question Meanyear
… in the past year? _____

▶ IF TOTAL IS ZERO, SKIP TO **SECTION IV** AND **Question Educ**

▶ IF TOTAL IS 1 OR MORE…
Within the last year which, if any, of the following has occurred as a consequence of your drinking?

	Has NOT happened	Happened once	Happened more than once	DK-NR
Question Injury Physical injury to yourself	1	2	3	99
Question InjOth Physical injury to others	1	2	3	99
Question Fighting Fighting	1	2	3	99
Question PropDam Damage to property	1	2	3	99
Question Absence Absence from work or school	1	2	3	99
Question PoorPerf Poor job or school performance	1	2	3	99
Question DamRelat Damaged friendships or relationships	1	2	3	99

Continued on following page

Question Memory Could not remember events or actions
that occurred while drinking   1   2   3   99

Question TypDays
On how many days in a typical month do you consume alcoholic beverages? _____

▶ TYPF IN THFIR ANSWER AND PRESS ENTER. USE 99 FOR DK OR NR.

Question TypNumb
When you consume alcohol, what is the typical number of drinks you consume at one time? _____

▶ TYPE IN THEIR ANSWER AND PRESS ENTER. USE 99 FOR DK OR NR. REMEMBER A DRINK IS ONE MIXED DRINK, ONE GLASS OF BEER, ONE GLASS OF WINE OR ONE SHOT.

Question TypHrs
Generally speaking, during a typical drinking occasion, what is the length of time, in hours, you
spend drinking? _____ hours

▶ TYPE IN THEIR ANSWER ROUNDED OFF TO THE NEAREST HOUR AND THEN PRESS ENTER. USE 99 FOR DK OR NR.

Question LastNumb
Think back to the last time you used alcohol: How many alcoholic drinks did you consume? _____

▶ TYPE IN THEIR ANSWER AND PRESS ENTER. USE 99 FOR DK OR NR.

Question LastHrs
Approximately how many hours did you drink? _____

▶ ROUND OFF TO THE NEAREST HOUR. TYPE IN THEIR ANSWER AND PRESS ENTER. USE 99 FOR DK OR NR.

Question LastDriv
Did you drive after this last drinking occasion?   1. Yes   2. No   99. DK-NR

▶ IF NO, DK or NR, SKIP To **Question Binge**.

Question HourDriv
How long was it after your last drink on that occasion before your drove? _____

▶ USE "0" FOR LESS THAN 30 MINUTES. ROUND OFF TO THE NEAREST HOUR. TYPE IN THEIR ANSWER AND PRESS ENTER. USE 99 FOR DK OR NR.

Question Binge
In the past 2 weeks, how often have you had... (IF FEMALE) ... 4 or more drinks in one sitting? _____
(IF MALE) ... 5 or more drinks in one sitting? _____

▶ TYPE IN THEIR ANSWER AND PRESS ENTER. USE 99 FOR DK-NR.

Question Dr1Hr
During the past month, have you driven within one hour after you have consumed 2 or more alcoholic beverages within an hour?

               1. Yes   2. No   99. DK-NR

Question YouDD
When you consume alcohol and know that later you will be riding in a car, WHAT PERCENT OF THE TIME do you make sure you have a designated non-drinking driver with you before you start drinking? _____

▶ TYPE IN THEIR ANSWER AND PRESS ENTER. USE 99 FOR DK-NR.

SECTION IV: DEMOGRAPHICS

That's it for the tough ones.... All we have left are a few questions so we can be sure our study is representative of a broad range of people.

Question Educ
What is the highest grade level of education you have completed? _____

▶ TYPE IN THEIR ANSWER AND PRESS ENTER. USE 16 FOR COLLEGE GRAD, 18 FOR MASTERS AND 20 FOR DOCTORATE. 99 IS DK-NR.

Question Student
Are you currently a student?
                                 1. Yes, full time college student
                                 2. Yes, part time college student
                                 3. Yes, high school student
                                 4. No
                                 99. DK-NR

Question Employed
Are you employed?
                                 1. Yes, full time
                                 2. Yes, part time
                                 3. No
                                 99. DK-NR

Question Drive
How many days do you drive in an average week? _____

▶ TYPE IN THEIR ANSWER FROM 0 TO 7. USE 99 FOR DK-NR.

Question SeatBelt
Did you wear a seat belt the last time you were in a vehicle either as a driver or passenger?

      1. Yes   2. No   99. DK-NR

Question Houshold
Which of the following best describes your household?

1. Live alone.
2. Live with spouse or partner.
3. Live with roommate(s).
4. Live with parents.
5. Other
6. DK-NR

Question Children
Do you have children living with you?   1. Yes   2. No   99. DK-NR

Question Weight
What is your approximate weight? _____

▶ USE 99 FOR DK-NR.

Question Height
How tall are you? _____

▶ ENTER THEIR HEIGHT IN INCHES. USE 99 FOR DK-NR.

4'10" = 58	5'2" = 62	5'6" = 66	5'10" = 70	6'2" = 74	6'6" = 78
4'11" = 59	5'3" = 63	5'7" = 67	5'11" = 71	6'3" = 75	6'7" = 79
5'0' = 60	5'4" = 64	5'8" = 68	6'0" = 72	6'4" = 76	6'8" = 80
5'1" = 61	5'5" = 65	5'9" = 69	6'1" = 73	6'5" = 77	6'9" = 81

Question Race
What is your ethnicity?

1. Caucasian
2. African American
3. Native American
4. Hispanic
5. Asian
6. Multiracial
7. Other
8. DK-NR

Question County
What county have you spent the most time living in during the last 6 months?

1. Beaverhead	16. Gallatin	31. Mineral	46. Sheridan
2. Bighorn	17. Garfield	32. Missoula	7. Silver Bow
3. Blaine	18. Glacier	33. Musselshell	48. Stillwater
4. Broadwater	19. Golden Valley	34. Park	49. Sweetgrass
5. Carbon	20. Granite	35. Petroleum	50. Teton
6. Carter	21. Hill	36. Philips	51. Toole

7. Cascade
8. Chouteau
9. Custer
10. Daniels
11. Dawson
12. Deer Lodge
13. Fallon
14. Fergus
15. Flathead

22. Jefferson
23. Judith Basin
24. Lake
25. Lewis and Clark
26. Liberty
27. Lincoln
28. McCone
29. Madison
30. Meagher

37. Pondera
38. Powder River
39. Powell
40. Prairie
41. Ravali
42. Richland
43. Roosevelt
44. Rosebud
45. Sanders

52. Treasure
53. Valley
54. Wheatland
55. Wibaux
56. Yellowstone
57. DK-NR

Question Reached

Is this where I have reached you for this call?　　1. Yes　　　　2. No　　　　99. DK-NR

Question Bye

That was the last question. Thank you very much for your time and cooperation. Goodbye and have a nice day/evening.

APPENDIX D
SAMPLE PHONE SURVEY SPECIFICATIONS

SERVICE: Conduct a telephone survey

PURPOSE: Survey will be used to collect data on self-reported perceptions and behavior regarding seatbelt usage in Montana adults.

REQUIREMENTS:

a.   Trained interviewers must complete 800, 10-minute telephone surveys.

b.   The survey must be conducted from June 1 to 11, 2003.

c.   Random Digit Dialing Sampling Technique, including unlisted telephone numbers, will be used.

d.   Sample will be composed of statewide Montana adults age 18 to 80.

e.   Sex and age of sample to be consistent with state demographic figures and proportionate to Montana county populations.

f.   Sample must be obtained by the contractor.

g.   Montana Social Norms Project will approve CATI programming script before survey begins.

h.   All call records must be coded and data will be returned to the Montana Social Norms Project in SPSS format with labels by June 18, 2003. Data report will include frequency distributions for each question.

i.   An electronic report of call disposition will be returned to the Montana Social Norms Project in Word format by June 18, 2003.

j.   Budget must contain all applicable costs including:

      i.   Cost per completed survey

      ii.   CATI programming

      iii.   Purchase of sample

      iv.   Record coding, SPSS data file and calling disposition report

      v.   Long distance charges

      vi.   Indirect costs and/or project administration costs

I, the undersigned, am over the age of eighteen (18) years or am granted permission by a parent or guardian and agree to the following:

1. I hereby irrevocably consent to the use by AGENCY, PROJECT NAME, their agents or assignees, the use of my name, biographical or occupational description, phrases regarding me, portrait, picture, likeness or voice in recording, videotape, television production or reproduction, sound track recording, film strip, film photography, CD-Rom, web site, or otherwise (all individually and collectively referred to a "Media").

2. I consent to the use of my name and biographical material, portrait, picture, likeness, or voice for informative purposes and for the advertising, publicizing, and exploitation of the Media. Such uses as may be made will not constitute a direct endorsement by me of any product or service.

3. I hereby grant to AGENCY, PROJECT NAME their successors, assigns, and anyone acting under the authority or permission of any of them, the right to make originals where appropriate and to use for any lawful purposes and reproduce in any form or manner and to copyright any of the Media referred to in the preceding paragraph.

4. Further, I waive all rights of inspection or approval, and I agree that such Media and all reproductions thereof, including, but not limited to, plates, negatives, videotapes, digital renderings, and exposed film connected therewith are and shall remain the property of AGENCY, PROJECT NAME.

Talent Name (please print): _____

Project Title: _____

Talent Signature: _____ **Date**: _____ / _____ / _____

Address (Street, City, State, Zip): _____

If the subject is a **minor** under the laws of the state where modeling, acting, or performing is done:

Guardian (please print): _____

Guardian (signature): _____ **Date**: _____ / _____ / _____

Address (Street, City, State, Zip): _____

Witnessed By (signature): _____ **Date**: _____ / _____ / _____

Witness Name (please print): _____

APPENDIX F

SAMPLE FOCUS GROUP/PILOT TESTING QUESTIONS

AGE _____   SEX _____

Do you drink alcoholic beverages? _____

If so, on average, how many alcoholic drinks per week do you have? _____

QUESTIONS ABOUT A TV COMMERCIAL

Please circle the number for each of the topics listed below that best describes your opinion about the commercial.
(1 = lowest; 5 = highest)

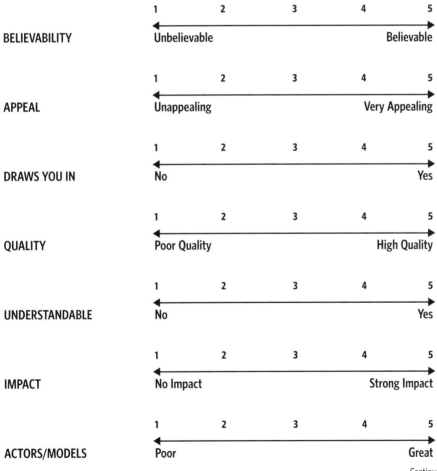

	1	2	3	4	5
BELIEVABILITY	Unbelievable				Believable
APPEAL	Unappealing				Very Appealing
DRAWS YOU IN	No				Yes
QUALITY	Poor Quality				High Quality
UNDERSTANDABLE	No				Yes
IMPACT	No Impact				Strong Impact
ACTORS/MODELS	Poor				Great

Continued on following page

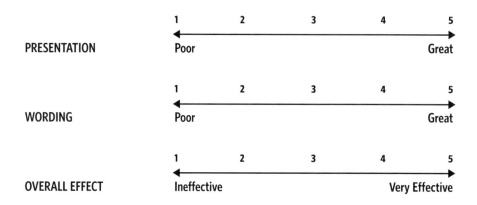

1. What is your initial reaction to this commercial?

2. What message is it trying to convey?

3. What do you think a person is supposed to do, if anything, as a result of this message?

4. Who is the target audience?

5. Is this ad effective? (Tone, images, pace, cast, script, lasting impression)

6. How could this ad be made more effective? / How would you change it?

7. Is there anything else you would like to say?

ADDITIONAL SAMPLE QUESTIONS

• Before today, were you familiar with this campaign?

• Where had you heard the campaign messages?

• What are you hearing people say about this campaign in your community?

• What outcomes or results from this campaign have you observed or heard about?

• What one thing do you like best about these materials?

• What one thing do you like the least?

• Were there any parts of this material that seemed inappropriate?

- If you could change one thing about the program, what would it be?

- How would you measure this campaign's success?

- Where do you typically get information about health-related topics?

- What places do you frequently go to where you might be open to receiving the campaign message (by looking at a poster or receiving a promotional item)?

- Are there any activities or promotions that could be run to encourage you to listen to the campaign message?

- (Describe a promotional idea.) What do you think of this method of getting the campaign message out?

- When you think about all the ideas that we have discussed today, what do you think is the most important for (name of organization) to do to get their message out?

- Have we missed anything?

I agree to participate in this focus group about _____ conducted on

_____ by _____.

I understand that the purpose of this focus group is to find out about _____

_____.

I understand that all the information I give will be kept confidential to the extent permitted by law, and that the names of the people in the focus group will be kept confidential.

I understand that my participation in this focus group is entirely voluntary, and that if I wish to leave, I may do so at any time, and that I do not need to give any reason or explanation for doing so.

I also understand that I have an obligation to respect the privacy of the other members of the group by not disclosing any personal information, comments or names they share during our discussion.

I have read and understand this information and I agree to take part in the focus group.

_____

your name (please print)

_____

your signature

_____

today's date

1. ASSEMBLE A CONTACT LIST

Include local media and community outreach outlets such as:

- ABC
- CBS
- NBC
- FOX
- UPN
- The WB
- Cable

- Radio stations
- Newspapers
- Regional Magazines
- Internet Sites
- Service Organizations

- Chamber of Commerce
- Government Offices
- Trade Associations
- Non-Profit Guides

For each of the above, gather the names, addresses, phone numbers, fax numbers and e-mails for all potential publicity personnel. Include:

- General Manager
- News Director
- Print Editor
- Promotion Editor
- Radio DJs

- Promotion Director
- Health/Traffic Reporters
- General Sales Manager
- Account Executives
- Public Service Director

2. INTRODUCE YOUR CAMPAIGN WITH A MAILING

Send your brochure and fact sheet to everyone on your contact list.

3. INTRODUCE YOURSELF ON THE TELEPHONE

Call each person on your contact list to introduce yourself and confirm that they received your materials. Ask for an appointment to meet in person to introduce your project, and provide specific information about your campaign and general information on driving after drinking.

4. SEND OUT A PRESS RELEASE

- Celebrities create coverage. Find a local or national celebrity (or a member of the media, such as the local newscaster or editor of the paper) to speak your message or emcee at an event. This almost guarantees coverage.

- Time your media coverage to relevant landmark events like the Superbowl or New Year's Eve

- Mondays and Tuesdays are "soft" news days. If you can target your events for these days, you'll have a better chance of coverage. Friday is typically the most difficult day to get coverage.

5. USE FREE PRESS

- Include your activities in the local event calendars put out by traditional and nontraditional media outlets. Try to give 2–3 weeks advance notice of any event. Use the press release strategy and follow up by telephone. Be sure the media have all of their facts correct.

- Organizations having events or fundraisers that tie in with local charities or service groups can go to the traditional media outlets for Public Service Announcements (PSAs). These can be created and placed free of charge.

6. INTRODUCE YOURSELF

- Hand-deliver promotional items.

- Invite a media person to be involved in your organization in a meaningful way.

An op-ed (so called because they are usually printed opposite the editorial page) is a signed opinion piece written by a non-reporter. Writing op-ed pieces can help bring attention to your campaign. Use an op-ed to explain why social norms is such a novel and promising approach to prevention, and why traditional approaches to prevention are not working. Don't forget to include facts and statistics to back up your argument.

Your op-ed should:

- Be timely and newsworthy
- Provide insight and educate the reader
- Be written for a general audience
- Highlight the issue and state your opinion in the opening paragraph
- Have a focused, clear editorial viewpoint; not ramble or unfold slowly like an essay
- Have a reasonable, informative tone
- Offer a solution or an alternative to the status quo
- Use powerful, direct language, emphasizing small words and vigorous verbs rather than adjectives and adverbs
- Avoid clichés, legal or academic jargon
- Include correctly spelled names and accurate statistics and facts
- Be typed, double-spaced and not exceed suggested length
- Include author's name, title and phone number at the bottom of the last page

Here are some guidelines for writing and submitting an op-ed:

Content and Length. 600 to 700 words is the typical length. Check with the editor of your paper to verify length requirements.

Capture. Hook them with your opening paragraph by leading off with your main point. Don't assume readers will read patiently through to the end while you build to the climax.

Speak Up. Op-eds are designed to express an opinion, not to provide neutral reporting. Op-eds should provoke discussion, controversy and response. Focus on one topic and have an opening and closing paragraph that clearly state your conclusion or opinion. Avoid the tendency to explain all sides of the issue.

Be Clear. Avoid clichés, unexplained acronyms, jargon, "legalese" or "academese." Op-eds appear in general-circulation publications and are designed for all audiences. Use simple, straightforward language and a conversational tone.

Be Accurate. Make sure that all of your facts and names have been verified and that there are no grammatical errors. Mistakes can hurt your credibility. Review the piece to ensure it flows well and does not contain leaps in logic.

Submission. You should submit your op-ed double-spaced with a suggested title, ready to print. Include a short (25 words or fewer) paragraph at the bottom describing the writer. Include the writer's name, phone number, background, relevant experience and/or credentials, and a photo or head shot. Call beforehand to encourage the paper to run your piece. If they do not run it the next week, call them again.

Cover Letter. You should include a short cover letter that highlights the most important aspects of the op-ed. Cover letters should accompany any op-ed submissions.

Your cover letter should include:

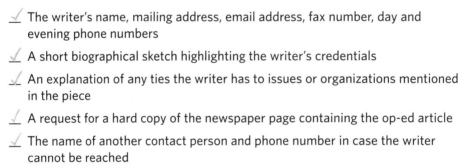

    ☑ The writer's name, mailing address, email address, fax number, day and evening phone numbers

    ☑ A short biographical sketch highlighting the writer's credentials

    ☑ An explanation of any ties the writer has to issues or organizations mentioned in the piece

    ☑ A request for a hard copy of the newspaper page containing the op-ed article

    ☑ The name of another contact person and phone number in case the writer cannot be reached

Montanans are ready for a 0.08 BAC law

by Jeff Linkenbach

[printed in the Billings Gazette 5/28/02 and in the Bozeman Chronicle 6/18/02]

Recent coverage of proposed changes in Montana's DUI law has raised the question of whether Montanans really support changes or whether political and financial pressure from the federal government has propelled change to the forefront. Discussion has also centered on using the law to influence social change—in this case, increasing the public's support for stricter DUI regulations and reducing the occurrence of drinking and driving among Montanans.

But the debate over stricter DUI laws misses an important point. An alternative scenario exists. What if the social change has already occurred, but it is the law that lags behind?

A recent editorial suggests letting the public decide on the proposed change from a 0.10 Blood Alcohol Content (BAC) legal limit to 0.08. The Montana Social Norms Project, a health promotion and education project at Montana State University, has already researched this very question. Preliminary results indicate that there is already strong support for a 0.08 law. More than two-thirds of young adults support the change from 0.10 to 0.08, according to a November 2001 survey of 1,000 Montanans aged 21 to 34.

Interestingly, this survey also reveals a misperception regarding others' support for this change. While the majority of young adults in Montana support the change, they do not believe their "peers" feel the same way. The same 1,000 respondents reported believing that, on average, only a third of 21- to 34-year-old Montanans would support changing the legal limit to 0.08. There is a nearly opposite relationship between what people support and what they think their peers support.

This type of misperception occurs with behavior as well. For example, the same survey revealed that while a large majority of Montana young adults, 4 out of 5, do not drink and drive, more than 90% of respondents believe that the average Montanan their age does.

The overall conclusion from this research is that although there is a misperception that drinking and driving is "normal" in Montana, the evidence indicates it is not. Further, despite a perceived resistance to stricter DUI laws, it appears there is strong support for them among the very segment of the population most likely to drink and drive—young adults. Older adults are likely to support the change as well because previous research shows that older segments of the population are more apt to support stricter laws in general.

Uncovering misperceptions helps explain how people might think there is widespread opposition to changing the legal BAC to 0.08. But when the reality of the healthy behavior that most of us engage in is made clear, suddenly the context surrounding these issues is altered. An accurate understanding of Montanans' beliefs and behaviors removes an assumed opposition and clears the path to establishing laws that accurately reflect the will of the public.

By realizing that these extreme negative behaviors are unacceptable and not as prevalent as we may think, we alter how we address these issues. Our efforts to implement prevention campaigns, to create useful policy and to form accurate opinions can benefit from the power of the majority who practice healthy, positive behaviors and who want our laws to reflect the same.

Any amount of driving after drinking is a serious problem that affects us all. One of the most powerful tools we have to address this concern is an understanding that the majority of Montanans support a strong response to drinking and driving.

We must set the record straight by replacing the misperception that Montanans do not support stricter DUI measures with the reality that most of us want to prevent drinking and driving.

Drinking and driving in Montana is a serious problem. Setting the legal BAC at 0.08 has saved lives in other states, and it will in Montana as well. It is a law we should implement, not to comply with a federal mandate or to change the culture of Montana, but because it would reflect the true behavior and the will of the people. Our culture is already there. Montanans are ready for a 0.08 law.

Jeff Linkenbach, Ed.D., is the director of the Montana Social Norms Project, home of the MOST of Us® Campaigns, and an assistant research professor in the Department of Health and Human Development at Montana State University.

Press releases are useful for communicating news about upcoming events, such as the implementation of a new prevention campaign or a public meeting.

Your press release should include pertinent, newsworthy information and anything you would like the public to know about. However, how the information actually appears depends upon the discretion of the editor. A phone call prior to submission might be helpful in making sure your most salient points are included.

The press release should be contain the following elements:

For Immediate Release. Always send out your press release when you are ready for it to be printed. Never ask for information to be held—if you are not ready to go public, don't send the release.

Contact. Include the name and phone number of the relevant person at your campaign.

Headline. Your headline should be no more than 20 words, bold and in caps. It should clearly summarize the focus of the story.

Location. Also known as the "slug," this is the geographic location from which your story originates.

Lead Sentence and Lead Paragraph. The lead sentence lists who, what, where, why and how. (Include how much if there is an entry or ticket fee.) This first paragraph should add supporting facts or relevant data to the opening statement, filling in further critical details.

Second Paragraph. The second paragraph is used to explain the situation further, sometimes restating it with a quote from the officials involved. Quotes are often used as a way of letting the story tell itself. This paragraph also begins providing background and filler information, a process that may continue for several paragraphs. It is a good idea to give a little more background or context/filler information than is absolutely necessary: this is deliberate "throw-away" material. Providing adequate background reduces the chances of the story appearing out of context.

Last Paragraph. Don't summarize the story; just let it end on its own. When you are finished, end with the journalism symbols # # # or -30- to signal the end of the release.

ACKNOWLEDGMENTS

This Toolkit represents the efforts and support of many different people.

The MOST Of Us Prevent Drinking and Driving Project was made possible by the financial and political support of the staff at the Montana Department of Transportation (MDT) Office of Highway Traffic Safety. These efforts began with Albert Goke in the early 1990s and continues today. Other key MDT staff that have made this project possible include Priscilla Sinclair, Audrey Allums, Jack Williams, Jim Erickson, Dave Galt, and Jim Lynch.

The project also received collaborative support from many other government officials from around the Big Sky State. Former Governor Marc Racicot trusted in this approach enough to film the first television commercial supporting it. Attorney General Mike McGrath supports the MOST of Us model from a perspective of strict law enforcement. The Montana Highway Patrol's leadership through Col. Paul Grimstad and Lt. Col. Mike Tooley is demonstrating how strong messages of law enforcement can be positive messages of social norms. Roland Mena of the Montana Board of Crime Control has supported this project through his key roles in preventing substance abuse in Montana.

The leadership of the National Highway Traffic Safety Administration (NHTSA) has been unwavering. At the NHTSA Region VIII office in Denver, Louis DeCarolis, Robert Weltzer, and Bill Watada have supported the MOST of Us project through our mutual conferences and trainings. The NHTSA staff in the Washington, D.C. office has been the anchor of this project's success and continued visibility. Ruth Esteban-Muir, Heidi Coleman, and DeCarlo Ciccel have provided the administrative and political foundation for this project to succeed and to evolve into something even bigger.

Social norms colleagues and consultants such as Wes Perkins, Bill DeJong, Koreen Johanesson, Michael Haines, and Alan Berkowitz have all played key roles in MOST of Us Prevent Drinking and Driving campaigns.

Finally, the biggest thanks goes to my many colleagues at Montana State University and the staff of MOST of Us who have supported this project in so many ways: Gary Lande, Jamie Cornish, Debbie Strachan, Geoff D'Atri, Stacey Scott, and Valerie Roche.

Thank you all for your contributions.

Jeffrey Linkenbach, Ed. D. is a research faculty member in the Department of Health & Human Development at Montana State University, and founding Director of the acclaimed MOST of Us Projects. Jeff is a well-known pioneer in the field of social norms and has a passion for developing innovative research projects that translate social science into social action. Dr. Linkenbach is responsible for developing the National Conference on the Social Norms Model and the Montana Institutes for Advanced Social Norms Practitioners. He has received several awards for his work, including the 2003 Public Service Award from the National Highway Traffic Safety Administration. He is an energetic presenter  whose technical expertise is widely utilized across North America. Jeff lives in Bozeman, Montana with his wife Cindy and their two children who bring joy and meaning to his work and life.